LA VIE EN FEMME

LA VIE EN FEMME

A GLIMPSE AT
THE RELATIONSHIP BETWEEN
GENDER, FEMINISM, AND SEX

ABIGAIL GLASGOW

NEW DEGREE PRESS

LA VIE EN FEMME

A Glimpse at the Relationship Between Gender, Feminism, and Sex

ISBN 978-1-64137-038-7 *Paperback*

ISBN 978-1-64137-039-4 *Ebook*

Try to learn to let what is unfair teach you.

—DAVID FOSTER WALLACE

To injustice that educates,

To women who elevate,

And to my mom, whose heart gets me out of bed every morning.

CONTENTS

CHAPTER 1

———

Gender is probably the most restricting force of American life.

—GLORIA STEINEM

PART I

SUNDAY, JUNE 14, 2015

Her face is stone; his words sporadic. I look back and forth between the three other women sitting at our kitchen table—three of my sisters, to be exact. Family style, as if we're about to share a meal. He flips our worlds upside down. Let me rewind.

I grew up with four sisters. The two oldest were my role models, the one right above me was my challenge, and the youngest was our godsend. We were a stock photo in a frame, a funny reality tv show, a Christmas card to put on the mantle. My mom stayed at home, my dad worked; we had a routine sprinkled with fun stories and minor upsets.

On this specific Sunday, I had received a text from my mom to be home by 5:30. This was out of character; with so many family members we all shuffled in at different times with little to no schedule, that's just how it was. Needless to say my suspicions arose. Pulling into the driveway, I saw my two oldest sisters; bizarre considering one lives in Maryland and the other has a family of her own. We all uncomfortably smiled—you know, that feeling when you know something is serious but you laugh anyway? It was like we were sitting front row at a funeral and could not stop laughing.

That day my dad revealed that he had been having an affair; the details at the time were ambiguous, but they have since come to light. The man who came to my plays, who told me bedtime stories, who held my mom's hand at my college tour–he was not who I thought he was. He was a reputation, a veneered smile; but he was not the dad I knew.

*   *

*Some people ask: 'Why the word feminist? Why not just say
you are a believer in human rights, or something like that?'
Because that would be dishonest. Feminism is, of course, part
of human rights in general—but to choose to use the vague
expression human rights is to deny the specific and particular
problem of gender. It would be a way of pretending that it was
not women who have, for centuries, been excluded. It would
be a way of denying that the problem of gender targets women.*

—CHIMAMANDA NGOZI ADICHIE

*   *

PART II

'I should point out, I am a feminist.'
One person in the audience cheers.
'Uh yeah, one person, that's all. That's the normal reaction.'

Quoted above, Michelle Wolf, contributor to *The Daily Show
with Trevor Noah*, sums up our current—albeit divided—state.
The politicization of this word reflects a two-sided narrative:
one of systemic rights and intersectional inclusivity, the other
of traditional values and economic mobility of the individual.
So, summarizing the popular consensus results in a perpetual

state of conflict and confusion. Hell, the effort to summarize the current state of my family would breed no popular consensus.

I recently stumbled upon a national survey conducted in 2016 by The Washington Post and the Kaiser Family Foundation that mirrors conversations, newscasts, and comedic sketches permeating discourse surrounding gender and equality over the past year. Tension surrounding feminism and what it includes or reflects is not simply a "battle of the sexes," but diverges at many points. According to their results, nearly 43% of people consider the word and/or the movement "angry," next to a 70% majority finding it to be "empowering;" and these statistics move across gender, race, socioeconomic status, etc. The evolution of this word and movement goes beyond its definition of a stride for equality; it has historical value that connects the Laverne Coxes to the Eleanor Roosevelts.

In the early 1900s, the word was casting votes and yellow sashes; it was Suffragettes marching. Post World War II, it was access to the workplace and Rosie the Riveter; it was women demanding they continue their lifestyles that were turned upside down when the labor arena said goodbye to soldiers. The first two waves are found in our textbooks. They are powerful, but they underline a subset of women: white, and middle-upper class to be specific. The third wave sought to redefine this F word. Through Ms. Magazine, personal essays of Gloria Steinem, and Anita Hill's stand against Clarence

Thomas, feminism sprouted into a variety of forms; intersectional forms, to be specific.

To define this term *intersectional* is more complicated, as it takes on different meanings depending on the narrator. I am a big define-colon-via-Google person, in which case intersectionality is the "interconnected nature of social categorizations such as race, class, and gender as they apply to a given individual or group, regarded as creating overlapping and interdependent systems of discrimination or disadvantage."

Who might fit into this movement? The answer is everyone: a transgender women of color, a pansexual jewish woman, a low-income woman who finds herself a writing a book to share a story.

Historically, storytelling has been the domain of the informer. The stories I hear through my headphones or through the lips of my educators are the ones that I remember. That is why I am equipped to write this book. Because I am a human who has felt these stories, heard these stories, or seen these stories. They touch me and the only way they can touch you is if you read them, swallow them.

My story stems from my family, and my inspiration from my gender.

PART III

"If you could choose your gender at birth, would you still pick woman?"

Every. Single. Time.

I realize that's easy for me to say. My intersection of identity is my gender and my socioeconomic status: I am a woman with little to no financial clout but a cultural capital that opens gateways of opportunities. So take this with a grain of salt.

I take pride in the idea of the *womyn*, in the reality of it all. I can wear my red lipstick with pride, pay my rent with pride (and government loans), and write this book with pride. All because, not in spite the fact that, I am a woman.

The beginning of this book starts with my truest encounter of pain and loss. Relative to some stories, it is quotidian; to others, it is foreign. In order to write a book about gender and its socialization or interpretations, I believe one should have a certain experience. I am 21 years old, so you might wonder what gives me experience.

As part of my role as an intern, I used to supervise the counseling sessions at HIPS—a harm reduction organization at 9th and H NE here in DC that popped my privileged bubble and taught me exactly why Georgetown lacks a metro. Miss Paula ran my favorite sessions. Her big voice booming, her contagious laugh breaking the tension of whatever heavy subject we were confronting that day.

On one particular Tuesday, for the session "Tuesdays with Miss Paula," the question of the day was "What was your most difficult moment on the streets?" I often tell this story to peers who ask me about HIPS; because it proves the non-judgmental, all-inclusive environment this gem of an organization provided. Each person shared their story. Words that made me tremble: Rape. Money from their night's work stolen. Gunpoint. Overdose. Narcan.

Then they circled back to me. "Okay sweetie your turn to share." I stared at them, and audibly laughed.

"I mean, come on," I found myself blurting. "What I experience is not *any* of these stories. It is a mild background. It's probably something you experienced that was a mild detail, not a life changing central plot."

"Everyone shares. That is our rule, and I can tell you've been through shit. So you share, honey, we know what you have to say is valuable."

Me. They saw what I had to say as valuable. That's more than I can say about many of my spaces. And that's the goal of this book. To create a space of empathy and connectivity when it comes to stories that might not otherwise be put next to one another.

You see, the current state is daunting. It is a compilation of waves and key words, of faces and protests. My current state in defining our world will not look like yours, but it will filter the conflicts of our divided opinions through stories of diverse individuals.

So, I am writing this book because I have a story; one that I believe reflects the harmful ways in which we internalize gender and carry those beliefs out via sex education, peer-to-peer interaction, and family life. The problem is a plethora of stories impregnated with differential mistreatment that have not yet been connected to one another. The problem is where divorce meets crude comments, where abstinence meets sexual harassment, where ignorance meets armpit hair.

It is not because of my religious values, my political beliefs, or even because of my personal relationships that I disagree with certain frameworks of gender and its ensuing issues in the United States. It is the stories, by and for women, that echo inside of me, that make me scream, that propel me to write these words. It is my friend who comes to me crying about a Chlamydia result. It is a mentor of mine who discusses the difficulty behind her abortion at age 22. It is my mother whose 63 year old tears I wipe after two years of divorce, loss, and suicide. Every story I hope to tell connects in *some* way to a misguided system that denies the resources to *all* students, but women especially, to pursue a safe and successful life. Our access (or lack thereof) to information challenges our perspective and redesigns our lenses; our lenses shape our attitudes, and our attitudes change the world. So I encourage you to flip through these pages in the hopes that you hear a new story, learn a new fact, or even see yourself reflected in a paragraph.

* *

Everyone deserves to feel whole. And each of us can do our part in expanding what it means to be a man for ourselves and the boys in our lives.

—THE MASK YOU LIVE IN

* *

PART IV

On November 12, 2017, Braxton Glasgow III committed suicide. That man, whose life had begun to decompose two years ago, and whose values were entrenched in dangerous notions of what it means to be a man, was my father.

I met Braxton Glasgow May 8, 1996. As you read above, I was born the fourth of five girls into what was deemed a picturesque family. We were by no means a cookie-cutter family. After all, most 7-person families defy generalization; but we were proud of what we had. Five vastly different personalities with two parental heads whose love story started February 3, 1979 on their first date and was still continuing well into 2015. Lauralee, my oldest sister, was our second mother. She spent her life being a stubborn badass, conquering her role as the oldest of five, nursing school, and now two daughters with fire inside them that mirrors their mother. Gracey, who follows, started checking our breathing before bed when she was 8. She was the one on guard during holidays, ready to take on the role of peacemaker when the time came. Our family conditioned her to mediate. As goes with the stereotypical middle child, Maggie went against the grain. She came along with a roller coaster of a temper and the ability to attract a room with her seductive appeal and powerful voice. My part of the story comes in later, but as author of this book I am sure you will soon learn that my ability to withhold my opinion is limited. Natalie, our last and most precious, observed all of our crazy stories and became our rock; she was our guardian angel, keeping us together with her kind heart and sprinkled jokes. All five of us are a product of the two who raised us: a woman whose bones exude empathy and a man whose sense of pride, when questioned, took his life.

PART V

Sex is innate; it is intimate; it is messy; it is beautiful; it is a weapon.

People are everywhere; they are close to you; they are unkind; they are life-changing.

Gender is automatic. We have deemed it a color, a toy, an identity and a role.

My sister called me recently, explaining that when she read this part of the book she immediately thought of our niece who turned four in late February.

"I went to buy Grace's birthday gift online by typing 'birthday gift for four year old.' Before I could finish the sentence, Google search provided me with search choices pertaining to the four year old's gender—i.e. boy or girl at the end of the search. And I just thought, huh, that's interesting. That literally from when someone is born you are pushing them into a direction; a direction not necessarily that they're opposing, but still, pushing them into this direction."

It's like our niece's friend who, at age 2, picked out a pink unicorn in the Toys R Us. His parents bought it for him, because he loved it, but it was mainly for a good laugh. Had he continued to want unicorns I would guess that by age 5 those unicorns would turn into tractors.

The intersection of sex, gender, and people is where this book will take you. Through your own experience reflected on pages of others. Your favorite sexual experience challenged by the toxins of others. My father's memory or my mother's strength echoing those from your own life.

This is not a how-to book. The fact of the matter is, there is no how-to when it comes to this topic. But there is a level of empathy that comes from exposing yourself to others and learning how to be vulnerable when hearing their struggles.

This book is for educators who want to change the dynamic of a classroom; for the young boys whose respect of women could be more tangible and less abstract; for the parents and grandparents who don't quite understand their crazy liberal college relative; and most of all, this book is for women who could find solace in stories and words that are identical or completely foreign to their own.

Why read this book? I have a story I would like to share, and I know that whoever may read this might too. I want people to read this and have it resonate; to read this and maybe go outside of their me bubble and feel what someone else does. I want my 80 year old grandmother to read the story of a trans woman of color and understand why she chooses to be a sex worker. I want my oldest sister to read the story of a president's quote and understand why I tremble when he speaks. I want my mother to read the story of her and understand why she is my feminist icon.

I hope I can embolden you—to stand up, to vocalize, to laugh, to cry. No matter your gender, your race, your religion, your ethnicity, your laundry list of *anything*, I hope you pick up this book and smile, and feel.

If you've made it this far and decide to stop or keep going, thank you either way for getting to know me in these words.

CHAPTER 2

――――

Do you remember when you believed in Santa Claus? For some, he was an integral part of their identity.

If you're like me, you knew Santa was not real at a very young age. Yes, I was the know-it-all who wanted to ruin Christmas for everyone in second grade because I was annoyed that my peers still obsessed over how one man made it to every home in one night.

Our exposure to certain sets of truths—or in the case of Santa, non-truths—creates a world within our world. A world of reindeer and elves and red suits. And these worlds shape our identity.

One's attitudes about Santa stem from a fantasy created by their parents. Now, replace the word Santa with sex and the word fantasy with construct. One's attitudes about sex stem from a construct created by their parents.

* *

Understand that sexuality is as wide as the sea. Understand that your morality is not law. Understand that we are you. Understand that if we decide to have sex whether safe, safer, or unsafe, it is our decision and you have no rights in our lovemaking.

—DEREK JARMAN

* *

PART I

Finishing high school in 1973, Becky Glasgow's stories consumed my curiosity; not merely because she happens to have birthed me, but because the mental pictures she painted were... for lack of a better word, whack.

"In my generation... everybody knew, was taught, [and/or] believed that you waited until you were married to have sex. That was just understood."

Growing up in Louisiana, the "belt buckle of the Bible" so they say, "that's just what girls believed in; so you didn't talk about it with your best friend."

Perusing the Louisiana State Archives, as one does, I came across a news coverage entitled *Louisiana: The State We're In* from 1979 about sex education in public schools. The debate revolved around creating a separate course exclusively devoted to sexual education with the argument being higher recognition of a student's "right to know." The alternative, and more strongly supported bill, mandated sexual education be taught within the confines of a health and wellness course; and underlined a parent's right to determine their child's exposure to sexual education. Amongst the oversize reading glasses and strapping business attire, a phrase struck me:

[Sex Education]: a topic that makes controversial as a descriptive adjective look inadequate.

So sex was as follows: for marriage, between a man and a woman, behind closed doors, and beyond controversial. Unfortunately, it is presented this way in 2018 across arenas and histories.

I asked, "so what about with your parents, what did that conversation look like?"

Mom said, "I remember there was a party at Becky L's house when I was in 10th grade. My mother drove me. She did not like Becky L because Becky L's mother was divorced and let her have parties. As she was dropping me off she said something about the birds and the bees and that was the end of that."

I think back to my experience with this sort of discussion. My mom had always encouraged us to wait, but it was not completely contextualized by the Bible. It was to protect me; she did not want me to feel the deep sense of shame or regret that many of us feel after an encounter that does not respect our fantasy or mere desire of what sex looks like.

So then I asked, "what about college?"

My mom was 17 years old when she stepped foot on Louisiana State University's campus. A literal *child*.

Talking about a girl who was also in my mom's sorority, she said, "I remember a younger girl in a younger sorority pledge class of Delta Delta Delta (TriDelt) at LSU. When she was rushing, the 'big stink around her' was well known...she had had sex with several guys. So her fellow sorority sisters were questioning whether she should be accepted."

I felt tears come to my eyes, sitting on the kitchen floor listening to my mom say this on the phone. What if this girl had been a fly on the wall during that meeting? If she had heard the words used by other women to describe her body, her actions, her morality? I pause.

"Why did they care?"

"If you did have sex you kept it quiet. . . because that was the culture."

So here were her tools when faced with questions of sex: a birds and the bees talk and the Church; because she could not even consult her friends for fear of being the hot gossip with a scarlet letter. There was shame, there was fear, and there was nowhere to go and no one to consult.

The construct of sex in my mother's world traveled from her own mother's words to a sorority bid; and unlike Santa, these values took on a tangibly consequential form.

Fast forward. Becky Glasgow is one of the highest paid female journalists in Louisiana in 1982. She has met a man with a charming smile (pre-veneers. . . in fact, he had a gap in his two front teeth) at a wedding. Within the year, they were married; her mobility was forever changed.

There's a little anecdote that I always refer to. Someone approaches a number of young, unmarried men and women to ask about how they see their futures. In summary, there are two distinct responses.

MEN: Yes, I want to get married, have children, and have a successful career.

WOMEN: Yes, I want to get married and have children, but I would love to have a successful career. *But.*

This charmed smile got a job in Richmond, Virginia. Becky Glasgow had a choice, but did she?

"I thought I had sacrificed because of my devotion to my family . . . to support his career," as many narratives of this generation go.

In retrospect, she describes a level of manipulation into leaving a career in journalism, but she believed she had truly chosen. So they uprooted from Shreveport, Louisiana with their family—at the time two parents and one daughter—to a place where she knew no one, and therefore had no local support.

"*FIVE* daughters?! Wow, your poor dad."

I have heard this exclamation hundreds of times *easily* when people react to the composition of my family. It used to make me laugh, except for the fact that, if you think about it, it's insulting. Of course its gendered. I mean it's insinuating that five daughters would be way too much for a father to handle... which is bullshit. I have *never* heard the comment "your poor mom," even though she carried us in the womb for 9 months. And no, we were not an easy bunch by any means.

Fast forward again. We are sitting on a small porch outside of my grandmother's home in a small neighborhood composed of many grandparents. It eerily reminds me of the opening scene of *Get Out* when the man is walking through a quiet, suburban neighborhood and you can feel his chills. This has become our home after a foreclosed home and the loss of a man we knew. Thankful that we had a roof to go to, we moved in with my mother's mother, and our family of 5 girls and a mother continue to navigate a two bedroom floor (as many have done). My mom is discussing her life since separating from my dad.

"I'll go to change a song on the radio because *he* didn't like it. But I realize, wait, I like this song." She points to her newly painted pink nails.

"You know, I've never painted my nails a color."

"Why is that?"

Because my dad did not like color on women. So my mother chose—this being the key word—not to wear colored nail polish.

What was choice in this relationship? What was choice in many relationships like this one? Perhaps nail polish color seems trivial, as there are many who would prefer that narrative to their own, but it reflects our ingrained gender attitudes that started with a conversation, or lack thereof, in Becky L's driveway.

* *

The problem with gender is that it prescribes how we should be rather than recognizing how we are. Imagine how much happier we would be, how much freer to be our true individual selves, if we didn't have the weight of gender expectations.

—CHIMAMANDA NGOZI ADICHIE

* *

PART II

Man Child: A Black Lesbian's Feminist Response, in the words of Professor Michelle Ohnona:

I was reading a piece by Audre Lorde about parenting. I always learn like fifty new things every time I reread her essays. In this particular piece, she talks about her struggles as a lesbian in a biracial relationship [and] how she struggles with what it means to be raising a man in this world and to be playing a big part in his socialization.

I asked about Ohnona's experience as a parent when I interviewed her back in the fall, only a few months ago. She spoke of Audre Lorde's wisdom, and how it translates into how she has observed parenting:

> [With kids] growing like crazy, hungry all of the time, [it's important to] try to find ways of signaling to [them] to be thoughtful, and that thoughtfulness is a gendered thing. We teach girls to be more mindful in the names of others.

Ohnona talked about how to be creative in parenting when it intersected with sexual education. She sees hunger for example, even at a young age, serving as a parallel of intense desire, sexual or otherwise. So in the same way it comes about in teaching kids to temper that hunger, she was communicating how one navigates controlling their impulses in situations where it feels incredibly difficult to control oneself (i.e. sex, consent, general respect etc.); and the goal here was to juxtapose this education against the heteronormative structure behind other sorts of parenting.

I really think that there is an appropriate age to talk to kids about consent and what that looks like for them in their world; tickling, play fighting, those are really teachable moments where you can talk to kids about how to check in with others about their physical and emotional boundaries, and what it means if you've crossed a boundary.

Audre Lorde and Michelle Ohnona hold in common their experiences as mothers within a queer world, and attempt to engage children in a productive and informative education.

"There are ways of laying groundwork for that really important conversation." Here, Ohnona again.

Groundwork for Ohnona are these conversations around the ways in which kids can be considerate and can understand consent. For Sarah Clements, groundwork was through books.

PART III

WINTER BREAK, 2016

Sarah Clements was cleaning out her room and the basement to help her parents declutter, as I'm sure we have all done at some point or another.

"They were going through a lot of books. My parents were both teachers, my dad a poet and writer as well, so I had always been surrounded by books; and this was such a privilege."

Clements came across a pile of picture books she read as a kid.

"Our family was a feminist family...there's no doubt that I grew up in a feminist context...[so I found books] about powerful women, about racial injustice; one was this gorgeous picture book about Martin Luther King Jr."

She realized how ingrained activism and feminism had been in her upbringing. This had so integrally determined her view on the world, her path as a high schooler and undergrad, and it had all started with images that, as a child, her parents handed over through bounded pages; much like Ohnona at the dinner table paralleling hunger to consent with her son.

"My family intentionally taught me these lessons as a kid so that when I grew up there was no doubt in my mind that I stood for these certain values."

It's no wonder that Clements has become an icon for social justice. Sitting beside her in an Uber after a dinner in Southeast DC, I picked her brain about sexual education and its intersection with her activism. With a background defined by honest information about the world, I wondered how she saw our generation's exposure to sexuality—whether at home, at school, or amongst ourselves.

"In college, we are influenced by [sexual] norms that are very much not real," she said.

If you're not having sex, well everyone else is. If you are, well no one is having it *that* much so maybe you should reconsider your behavior. Do you need condoms? Well, the University does not provide them, but they do sell pregnancy tests.

As young women on a college campus, we are navigating a confusing line. And as low income students on this campus, our contradicting line becomes a corner that has little to no access—to resources such as condoms or STI tests, or even access to information essential to being a sexual being at college. We have a tendency to both reduce the category of gender and simultaneously ignore the intersectional pieces of age, socioeconomic status, race, etc. that further inhibit mobility; by this I mean the ways in which these elements of identity gives us opportunity. I was recently speaking to a friend of mine who is a woman of color at a University business school:

> I am the only black woman in my class, and that filters how I interact with my classmates. If I become too angry, I'm the stereotype that is 'the angry black woman,' but if I don't speak up, I'm assumed to be unintelligent.

So here, her race has a huge impact on opportunities within the classroom because of how *others* inhibit her mobility by assuming that her race reflects her intelligence. In terms of sexual education, many portions of one's identity mold the ways in which we interact with sex; and this thus changes our relationship with sex, in some cases in an unfair or false manner.

So to expand upon Clements' quote, we are influenced—here I'm speaking specifically about the University level—by sexual, racial, economic, religious, and other norms that are *very much not real;* because of this, this false information distorts our reality, thereby convoluting our attitudes and actions.

The main takeaway? We wrongfully define equality and progress and shuffle these ideas into a narrow tunnel, one of white walls and male gazes. In other words, my main message here is the primordial role upbringing plays in defining identity; and if your upbringing is defined by said white walls and male gazes—or anything that has a specific structure in terms of expectation—it will distort identity.

Michelle Ohnona put it best:

> The biggest pitfall that I think is sort of threatening us is this idea that equality or progress is about one person's success, paycheck, [and/or] degree; as opposed to looking

at systems, at trends. And if we think about it, if we were physicists and were trying to prove something we would never look at just one instance, [or] one experiment, we would look at a trend, a corpus, a body; and so I am very concerned about the approach to all issues but in this instance gender equality where it becomes about [only] one woman" or one layer, or race, or status of women.

And even if you're not the extreme, anti-sexual discourse mindset, you could still harm the progress of pro-sexuality mentalities.

When on the phone with Helen Brosnan, a friend and mentor throughout my time at college, we talked about our self-perceptions of sexuality that stemmed from our upbringing.

"I probably had a very rigid notion of identity and understanding myself and what I thought . . . equalled a successful, happy person," she said when comparing herself as a student to now, almost three years out.

"University can be pretty rigid and maybe sometimes one-dimensional in what it overtly presents as self-actualized. Not necessarily *regressive,* but one-sided."

She painted parallels between discovering feminism and discovering sexuality.

It literally took me four years of a frankly radical thought transformation and people teaching me and me educating myself; a lot of women of color teaching me and saying it's more complex than that. It took me 4 to 5 years of college/post college to go through the transformation of the struggles/complexity of feminism, and that parallels my experience with sexuality.

Because sometimes, even those of us who see ourselves as all-knowing when it comes to this or that subject, we need a wake up call from those living in different worlds to show us what is missing.

"This speaks to the value of going out of your way to make sure that people you interact with on a daily basis reflect diversity," Brosnan underlined.

From elementary school to graduate studies, we are loaded with constructs. From Becky L's driveway, to Ohnona's kitchen table, to Sarah Clements' basement to Helen Brosnan's post-grad reflection, we have an obscure web of sex attitudes.

Like Gloria Steinem says, "you can directly predict the amount of democracy of a society by the amount of democracy in the home."

CHAPTER 3

———

PART I

*At one point she said 'how many of you don't know the word
vulva here'. . . and then she said:*

*Think about the number of boys your age who don't know the
word penis. What boy who has learned how to speak does
not know the word penis?'*

*And [yet] we as women at this liberal feminist education
still. . . did not know what you were referring to when you
say vagina. . . [versus] your vulva.*

I'm sitting across from my friend Anita. It's our typical Sunday
where we avoid work and talk about our frustrations. We

get into her upbringing at Chapin, an all girls school on the Upper East Side of Manhattan, 84th and East Avenue to be exact. She beams as she talks about her hip, young sex ed teacher whose words I just quoted above, and I think about my last week sitting in Psychology of Sexuality as a senior at Georgetown University. We had just gone over the anatomy of the penis and the vulva—yes, the vulva; because the *vulva* is the external genital structure of a woman, and the *vagina* is the internal organ. How many classmates of mine did not know that? Well, I won't out them; but let's just say in a room of highly educated 21 year olds, a disturbing amount could not accurately label a body part they've known about since birth.

So, without further ado:

A PERSON'S GUIDE TO THE FEMALE ANATOMY: A SUMMARY

Please note this bulleted list is limited to the sexual organ prescribed for the female *sex*, not gender.

PARTS OF THE EXTERNAL STRUCTURE

- The vulva is also referred to as the pudendum in scientific circles; a gerundive of the Latin word pudēre—"to be ashamed."

- The Labia Majora, or "outer lips," encases the external genital structure; while the Labia Minora the "inner lips" encases the internal structure
- The prepuce is the clitoral hood, similar to the male foreskin
- The clitoris is the go-to point for sexual arousal; in fact, woman often reach orgasm more frequently via clitoral-stimulation than the traditional penetrative model we are often taught (Fugl, Meyer, et al. 2006). Why not throw in a little APA citation just for kicks.

PARTS OF THE INTERNAL STRUCTURE

- The introitus, or vaginal opening; I had never heard this word before my aforementioned Psych of Sexuality course.
- The hymen covers the introitus until broken, and this comes with a story; because you see the hymen has a direct relationship with a woman's virginity. In many cultures, if a woman is raped, she will undergo hymen repair in order to reduce shame and restore virginity before marriage. Located in Queens, Esmeralda Venegas has deemed herself "Queen of the Virginity" because of her position involving hymen repair at the Ridgewood Health and Beauty Center.
- The vagina is strictly the internal genital structure that extends from the introitus to the uterus.
- The Grafenberg spot, commonly known as the G-spot or by some as the "gynelogical UFO", actually does not have

a defined location. Some experts believe that research surrounding this area is unnecessary, due to the role of the clitoris as a center for pleasure; then again, other's believe the lack of research surrounding an arena of female pleasure is reflective of a society that prioritizes the pleasure of one gender over another.

- The cervix is the lower portion of the uterus, and the gateway to sperm.
- And finally the famous uterus, which protects the fetus during pregnancy and is the protagonist in menstruation.

So here's a quiz: how many of these structures did you know? No judgment, just think about it.

This is our country's problem. We have all, to some extent, interacted with sex; it is quite literally unavoidable. You, sitting in your chair at this moment, came from sex. It might not have been a conventional process, but sex was involved. Perhaps you have sex, read about sex, or have seen sex on your screen. Sex permeates our lives *all of the time*; and yet University students do not know what a vulva is, one cannot say the word vagina in a restaurant above a whisper without stares, and, most importantly no two people's sex education in the United States resembles the other. So the above outline could be yesterday's news or a newfound puzzle, depending on who you are.

PART II

That is why when you're watching a movie and there's a sex scene, everyone becomes motionless, and silently begs for the merciful release of death.

Sex is a word we mumble in public settings; an action that occurs behind closed doors; a history that underlines issues of culture and politics from the Ancient Greeks to the current administration. In 2015, John Oliver on Last Week Tonight gave America the sex talk we needed to hear. His words quoted above could not be more accurate. Through stories and statistics, he explained our relationship with the concept of sex. We avoid it like the plague, we deny its existence, and historically we have passed laws constructing how it can exist. Societal norms have blindly accepted restraints on sex and the discomfort around it without questioning the detriments of such an acceptance.

When I reflect back on my sex education, I picture a beautiful, white, blonde volleyball coach writing the word A-B-S-T-I-N-E-N-C-E on the board for myself and my fellow 8th grade female peers. I remember this woman preaching to us about outlets outside of sex. She highlighted bonding activities she and her partner enjoyed like doing the laundry or cooking meals for the week together. I remember praying my sex life did not look like hers. That's not to devalue laundry and cooking with one's partner; but that is to say that 8th grade Abigail—who fantasized over her first kiss and envied Jennifer

Garner in *13 Going on 30*—wanted to know the ins and outs of what this hushed concept actually was.

Rewind about 45 years, and a different 8th grader was sitting in a room perhaps watching the 1966 film *Parent to Child About Sex*. While the riveting title might have you on the edge of your seat, the content is merely an uncomfortable back and forth between parents and their children shown in classrooms in hopes of instructing any viewer about how to discuss and understand sex. While you might chuckle at the thought of this film being showed today, its premise is not far off from what some systems—be it school or family or otherwise—encourage or teach.

In fact, according to the *Guttmacher Institute State Policies Brief* published in August, 2015, only 22 states mandate that students have some level of sexual education; more strikingly so, only 13 states require that the instruction be medically accurate. So, to deconstruct this, even when states require sexual education, it is not necessary they be accurate *nor* is it pertinent that they cover certain material. That is to say, some 15 year olds are learning about their own genitals, about effective contraception and sexual activities, and about options available in the case of pregnancy or an STI (Sexually Transmitted Infection); while their state neighbors' sex ed is limited to poems of abstinence, horror stories of premarital sex, and analogies that compare sexually active women to dirty shoes. It is this roller coaster of exposure to information that affects our attitudes; and our attitudes that affect the way we see others and the world.

If you're a 17 year old girl attending a public school in Mississippi when the state passes its first education law in July of 2013, you have never seen a condom demonstration in your sex education class. You somewhat understand the banana imagery laughed about amongst your friends, but when you find yourself about to have sex, you might not know what exactly safe sex looks like *physically;* in fact, if you've never had any sort of condom education, you and your partner might not even *own* condoms much less know how to use them. So this would explain *Mississippi Adolescent Reproductive Health Facts* which ranks Mississippi as the number two state in the country in terms of teen pregnancy rates.

And this does not strictly disadvantage women. A friend of mine recounted a comedic yet devastating story of how his friend's Arizona education ended up harming his sex life:

> A good friend of mine told me a story of the first times he had sex. . .that he hated it. . .he was a junior in high school. He and his girlfriend did it again because it hurt HIM so badly and he thought 'maybe the rumor about it hurting was true for me too'. . .it still hurt. In the post-sex boasting narrative with a friend, he asked if it was

supposed to hurt so badly. Long story short, my friend realized that he had been putting his testicles inside the condom too, causing massive pain.

If your 10th grade history professor only mentions Martin Luther King Jr. when discussing the Civil Rights Movement, you will not have the tools to discuss Malcolm X's philosophies. If your 1st grade math teacher blatantly leaves out even numbers during your lesson on addition, the number 8 is entirely foreign. If your art substitute decides to veer from the "artistically accurate" standard of colors, then you might think red plus white makes green and you'll get pink grass every time you choose to paint. The point being, to leave out certain facts and certain visuals, or to deny that any other options within a subject exist, is to disadvantage your pupil. To hope that your students just learn their times tables at home rather than in the classroom is a weak argument if you want them to be a successful mathematician, just as to reduce sexual education to the confines of one's home—defined by other factors such as religion—denies your student the tools to be safe when discussing or engaging in sex.

PART III

It was 8th grade biology with Mr. Gibson. I was late, and it was dark, so I had to sit in the front. I was sitting next to this kid Terrell, we played football together. Great guy. We were talking about XY chromosomes because I think that was what we were studying at the time, and all of a sudden there was a baby and its head crowning out of a vagina and no one in the room was okay. We were like oh my gosh THIS is what childbirth is? This is not magical. People were pretty caught off guard. I had to go to the bathroom because I got sick. It was super graphic. I would have been fine if he had told us it was going to happen.

Ramsey grew up in Fayetteville, Arkansas. His reaction to the fateful birthing video at McNair Middle School is the manifestation of a counterargument to a progressive sexual education framework. Many parents and educators find the information around sex to be graphic, inappropriate, or tempting. If you show your child what ice-cream looks like, they'll be tempted to taste it. That is why strategies and systems exist to resist an adolescent's desire; or, in Ramsey's case, to show them an outcome of sex that at age 13 could scare you away from sex altogether.

On May 22, 2015, *The Washington Post*, released an article sharing that Congress had just increased funding for programs that underlined abstinence until marriage to 75 million dollars. This kind of action puts a fiscal quantity on sex. It says that power, whether monetary or otherwise, is behind the analogy that compared Elizabeth Smart to a chewed up piece of gum. Abstinence-only curriculums preach every way a woman can say no, but do not highlight the other person involved. If you are driven to say no, this means the person with whom you are interacting did not *hear* nor *understand* your lack of consent; *this* is what these programs do not take into account. Pam Stenzel, a public speaker who stands center stage screaming "ABSOLUTELY NO GENITAL CONTACT OF ANY KIND," does not see that her words merely perpetuate a patriarchal structure wherein marginalized people—be it women, people of color, LGBTQ individuals, etc.—must repeatedly take responsibility when faced with someone who cannot *hear* or *understand* them. She does not see the link between her chant and that of Yale students in October of 2010 yelling "NO MEANS YES, YES MEANS ANAL!" Perhaps Stenzel sees a path to heaven, and these Yale students a path to sex; but both parties do not see the agency they steal from those who want to make a choice between yes and no.

Here is the outcome:

In the US, on average, adolescents have their first kiss at 15, and their first sexual intercourse experience at 17 (Reagan et al. 2004).

In the US, adolescents have higher rates of STIs and unintended pregnancies compared to other industrialized nations.

The thread from one fact of sexual activity to unintended consequences and infections is access to sexual education. According to study conducted in 2010 by researchers Mosher and Jones, there are about 6 explanations for this thread.

- 43.9% of heterosexual women did not believe they could get pregnant when not using contraception
- 22.8% of heterosexual women did not mind getting pregnant
- 16.2% of heterosexual women were concerned and or not educated surrounding the side effects of birth control
- 14.1% of heterosexual women did not expect to have sex
- 9.6% of heterosexual women said their male partner did not want to use contraception
- And 7.3% of heterosexual woman said their male partner did not want them, the woman, to use contraception

I'm scrolling through old classroom files about Psychology of Sexuality with Paul Merritt, and I think back to an interview I had in his office a few months back. I asked Merritt about what he observes when teaching students.

When I teach Psychology of Sexuality, students are way far behind. I had a student last year who didn't know her fertility changed over a 28 day cycle... [that's] insane that no one ever taught her or that she never thought to think about her body in that way. No one taught her about what the whole point of the menstrual cycle is... how did that happen?

This goes back to an ignorance surrounding the word vulva, and the above stats regarding unintended pregnancies. We know why and how veins pump blood through us, but we do not learn how our genitals work, which perpetuate a society, or so the Church and our elders tell us.

"It's almost like we're the most Victorian society on the planet in terms of our approach to sexuality, and it has gotten even worse."

I have a friend who attended The University of Notre Dame. If you didn't already know, it's a Catholic school. I had already heard her freshman adventure stories, but this one was particularly interesting.

> You can't pick up your birth control at the Walgreens...literally the primary pharmacy on campus *in* our health center...unless you have a written physician's note that says it's NOT for birth control purposes, but instead let's say for your skin. The Health Center also does not provide condoms...it's just not the right sex education.

I asked how she felt about this entire situation.

> I wasn't surprised, just because of all the rules we have on campus like with sex and gender...like I can't be in a

boy's dorm past midnight...so I wasn't surprised...I just didn't know they would prevent like...our medication.

And this is counterintuitive when given facts about contraception. This is Merritt again:

> Providing access to longterm contraceptives decreases teen pregnancy, decreases abortion rates by about 55% and yet [people] will push to not publicly fund contraception. You can't be anti-abortion and anti-birth control at the same time. They're logically inconsistent. That's my issue with this sort of anti-science initiative.

I mean think about it. The term has the word control in it. Birth *control*. Which, yes, is what it does, but there are other uses for it. Some women take it for acne, others for horrible period cramps, others even to regulate their period. So yes, while there are many people who use birth control in order to prevent pregnancy, there are other additional positive consequences for birth control. My sister posed the question, "What if we renamed it? I mean, what if we just referred to it as Ortho Tri-Cyclen lo or something, that way people don't think of it solely in terms of its relationship to pregnancy. Maybe it won't scare so many people away." This is the part of the book where I say directly to Gracey: you are far more brilliant than you even know.

I remember when I first brought up the topic of birth control to my mom. I was 18, I believe. It was something I had reflected on given the daunting four years ahead I would soon be confronting. Leaving my cozy home since I was little, I was nervous. Next to printed out pictures of friends from home, a hip new comforter, and a vast array of colorful pens, I figured birth control was essential to a "Intro to College Survival Pack." We talked about it briefly, and I laugh now because the blatant nature with which I discuss sex with my mom looks nothing like the timid, slightly skittish one we had before I uprooted.

But so a lot of this—"this" because talking about sex specifically within education—is about literacy. And it is necessary that our education framework include a certain level of sexual literacy that distinguishes sex education from sex socialization, and how the two intertwine and diverge. Socialization, according to Shtarkshall et al.'s *Sex Education and Sexual Socialization: Roles for Educators and Parents*, is the "process through which an individual acquires an understanding of ideas, beliefs and values, shared cultural symbols, meanings and codes of conduct." It is the reason we grow up encouraged to be modest and condemned in private or sexual spaces. It is the reason that within religious spaces, and consequently outside of them, we see sexuality as a divine gift. It is the reason why we avoid discussing birth control and other forms of contraception as they imply deviant behavior.

But we don't always see the fact that these terms and values are socialized and thus internalized, we see them as fact. Which is why we walk into Paul Merritt's classroom, or a building at Chapin, with Victorian tools.

CHAPTER 4

——

The following chapter is strictly about the vagina.

* *

No woman gets an orgasm from shining the kitchen floor.

—BETTY FRIEDAN

* *

PART I

Define: *Orgasm*

A climax of sexual excitement, characterized by feelings of pleasure.

Thank you, Google.

I sat last spring creating a word cloud. Certain words were larger than others, as that's how word clouds generally work. Sex. Noise. Fake. Gap. It was our second Psychology of Gender assignment. The three of us in my group had chosen the Orgasm Gap. I knew it existed because we talk about it after our stride of prides, after we watch a sex scene in a movie, we just talk about it. Or it just goes unsaid but we all understand; we being the many of my female peers at University, and beyond.

To get psychological with it, there exists a distinction between the male and female orgasm.

The male orgasm consists of "two phases: the emission phase and the ejaculation phase."

The female orgasm has been classified into two types: "surface orgasms or deep orgasms which are labeled by the individual according to distinguishable differences between the sensations and locations of each type" (Palmer 2014). The surface orgasms, which focus on the surface of the genitalia, are also referred to as clitoral orgasms; whereas the "deep" orgasms, which are associated with internal sensations, are commonly regarded as the more "mature" vaginal orgasm (Vance & Wagner, 1976). Researchers have sited stimulation of the clitoris as the leading source of pleasure that generates orgasm;

however, there are no distinguishable biological differences between clitoral and vaginal orgasms (Palmer 2014).

Ultimately there exists a gap among the sexes—and I use sex here rather than the word gender as I am discussing sexual organs—regarding frequency of orgasm. According to a national sample of men and women in the United States (Frederick 2017):

> Heterosexual men were most likely to say they usually-always orgasmed when sexually intimate (95%), followed by gay men (89%), bisexual men (88%), lesbian women (86%), bisexual women (66%), and heterosexual women (65%).

So why, then, is there not some arena where heterosexual men are talking about a silence of their partners' during sex? Because, in *When Harry Met Sally* style, fake orgasms are the outlet.

There's a scene in *When Harry Met Sally* that the famous line "I'll have what she's having" comes from. The two protagonists are sitting in a diner-style restaurant, talking about how Harry leaves many women the morning after he spends the night with a quick goodbye and a lie about a squash game.

As Sally questions him, he says "Why are you getting so upset? This is not about you."

To which she replies, "Yes it is. You are a human affront to all women and I am a woman."

They continue talking after Harry says that he's sure that the women still have a good time, even if he leaves quickly. Without actually using the word orgasm at first, the two discuss how Harry is confident that he pleases these women due to their vocalization during sex. Sally, chuckling, opens his eyes to the world of faking it. "Most women at one time or another have faked it," she says.

"And you don't think I could tell the difference?" He replies. Sally proceeds to loudly, and quite publicly, fake an orgasm. To which an onlooker says, "I'll have what she's having."

So it's very much a phenomenon.

An interesting finding included in the above national sample was that "41% of heterosexual men reported that their partner orgasms usually-always compared to 33% of heterosexual women reporting that they usually-always orgasm" (Frederick 2017). Researchers attribute part of this disparity in perception "to women faking orgasms" which may be done for a variety of reasons including "out of love for their partner, to protect partner self esteem, intoxication, or to bring the sexual encounter to an end" (Frederick 2017).

Theories of this range from sociocultural to biological, as psychology lectures often go. The social is most of this book. Sexual double standards and the like. There's the stigma around female pleasure, that dates back to the 1800s when the vibrator was created. The correlation of health and sexual pleasure manifested through symptoms such as fatigue and anxiety; i.e. women were not orgasming. Diagnosed with "female hysteria," women were often prescribed pelvic massages which lead them to orgasm.

About a year ago, I sat wide eyed after a performance of *The Vibrator Play*. It was the first I had heard of this medicalization of female pleasure in a way that made me laugh but also made me pause. Because the reality is we still haven't quite gotten a hold of what female pleasure looks like. This period of history is one often mentioned by psychologists when describing how we place female pleasure into the hands of male scholars.

I spoke to the actor who played the doctor–whose goal was to "cure" female "hysteria"—about what he discovered:

> I mean I guess the thing that struck me most about the play is the world of sexuality and how often the freedom of sexuality has been taken away from women and left being deciphered by... men, who often lack a sense of their own sexuality. In the play for instance, it takes the entirety of [it] for [the doctor] to feel comfortable to

engage with his wife sexually. She desperately wants to know that her sexual drive and desires are prioritized over her husband's patients. But they're not.

The stigma that was explained on the Davis Performing Arts Center stage—a construct that pushes against female pleasure and the existence of sex as pleasurable at all—pervades social attitudes and a lack of education surrounding the orgasm.

Back to theories. One that always makes its way to the forefront of a psychology lecture is the adaptationist theory. This particular theory references the evolutionary purpose of orgasms as a mode evolutionarily engrained in males and females to potentially explain the disparity. On the one hand, the male's reproductive potential is not constrained by age, and thus "the orgasm rewards men for ejaculating and for seeking intercourse with a greater number or variety of reproductive opportunities" (Frederick 2017). On the other hand, the female orgasm provides an adaptive function as it "facilitates bonding with a long term romantic partner and promotes reproduction with males with heritable traits that can be passed onto offspring" (Frederick 2017). These hypotheses aim to explain how the female orgasm is impregnated with context—relational status and partner characteristics—more so than that of the male, explaining why the frequency of female orgasm is lower among women than among men.

Ultimately, the findings of the national sample collecting orgasm frequency data provides that there may be biological factors that make male orgasm easier than female orgasm but also indicate that the gap can be reduced by "addressing sociocultural factors and by encouraging a wider variety of activities when men and women are sexually intimate."

Ultimately, so much of this revolves around education. Whether that comes in the form of my peers on stage, or a conversation with a partner. Otherwise, a lot of us might be Sally for more than one film scene.

* *

Even if times are tough and you're enduring a terrible heartache, it's important to focus your anger on a vibrator, not another person.

—CHELSEA HANDLER

* *

PART II

And then she said "you know, have you ever liked, touched yourself between your legs... and like do you know how it feels... you know how it starts feeling good?"

I was chatting with a mentor of mine about her dual role as a parent and educator. She opened with the line above, discussing how her daughter had just described masturbating and coming to orgasm "in more detail than [she'd] ever heard in [her] life."

Masturbation. Say it a few times and see if you get uncomfortable. If you say it at the dinner table, your grandma might have to wash your mouth out with soap. If you say it amongst friends—well, that depends. I knew all my guy friends did it. They talked about pornography as if it were some claim to fame. But when it came to girls, this was another story. I think back to conversations in high school that tiptoed around what we wanted to ask: do you do it? Is it weird if I do?

At age 5, my mentor's daughter openly spoke about an experience. She asked the right questions, and explored her boundaries. For the purpose of protecting anonymity, I have not used their names.

"That's great! I'm so glad you're discovering your body, this sounds like something you should do in your room. It's all great, just don't forget to be in your room..."

But for most of us, it doesn't go that way. It's a confused look from a fellow female; a shush from a sibling or parent; or a "oh that's hot" from a guy friend who reconstructs your exploration into his own pleasure.

"She completely freaked me out...I have only once in my entire parenting life...been like I can't do this...and was not making eye contact."

Yes, self-pleasure is not the best table topic; not the easiest conversation for a morning stroll. But it exists, for everyone, in some capacity. We preach self care, but when that becomes sexual, we shy away from it or denounce it as deviant. We laugh about it with the middle school boys, but when it becomes something for girls as well, we put a taboo label on it.

The sexual education system is doing its students a disservice by not providing them with the tools on understanding anatomy and pleasure in an individual way. Masturbation is a wellness activity that has proactively been excluded from an agenda made to better the health of students; and by not talking about it, we put the responsibility solely on parents navigating education at home, or amongst friends whose lack of sexual education should not determine anyone else's gain.

"And I thought, well, you win. I am now completely embarrassed."

PART III

Warning: the following excerpt is about theories behind Feminist Thought and gets pretty academic. It reads like a mini journal entry for a class (because, well, that's where it came from).

When I took Intro to Linguistics my freshman fall, I left knowing what a discourse marker was and thinking that would be the extent of its applicability. I took it because, at the time, it was a prerequisite for my French major; it no longer is, but I am content with my introduction. Because I've noticed the *integral* role linguistics plays in both the micro and macro picture.

For instance, if my niece were to say the word vagina out loud in the family room, she would be condemned. The penis game, however, is one with which many of us are familiar (it's when you go back and forth with friends seeing how loud you can get saying the word Penis without a. feeling embarrassed or b. getting noticed). This is a mini case study on linguistics; how the mere use of a word reflects an attitude toward a specific gender, a shame associated with the female body and, alternatively, a pride associated with the male body.

I used the word vagina a lot in my college courses. Mostly, because it was relevant; and a part of me will admit it was fun.

When I was a sophomore at Georgetown, I joined an organization called the Lecture Fund. This is a group of students whose mission is to invite people to campus to spark dialogue. I joined because I wanted to get more involved in the agency behind inviting and thus bringing new people to Georgetown; specifically in the hopes of diversifying the content of those who came to speak. My first (and only) speaker that I hosted was Fuambai Ahmadu.

At the time, I was taking a class for my Women's and Gender Studies major entitled International Women's Rights. It was my first of many entry points into global feminism; and how we conflate definitions of the Woman, as very much expanded upon by theorist Mohanty in her piece entitled *Under Western Eyes*. The course I took covered an intro to many subjects— veiling, female circumcision, rape as a weapon of war, etc.—and contributes strongly to one of Mohanty's elaborations on how we pre-configure or pre-define non-Western women before we have any concept of them inside of social networks and relations.

It was in this class that I first truly questioned the construct of the Middle East that had been shoved down my throat in Richmond, Virginia by a white, Southern demographic. I knew that generalizations of Islam as a religion were falsely fabricated, but I did not know to what extent; I knew that I found George W. Bush's decisions in relation to the War in Afghanistan as problematic, but again I did not know to what extent. This course gave me the tools to continue to deconstruct how the reality I had been handed was in fact not at all a reality, but the "white men save brown women from brown men" metaphor made tangible.

So, back to Fuambai Ahmadu.

I reached out to her as we had just read one of her responses to the Western notion, more specifically linguistic choice, of "FGM," female genital mutilation. Up until Omar's class, I had not questioned this terminology. I pictured what my culture wanted me to picture: some random, uneducated doctor sewing together the labia of a young woman against her consent to strip her of her pleasure and agency. This is obviously (or I guess not so obviously, depending on how you are exposed to this term) not the case. Fuambai Ahmadu was an interesting author as she was born and raised in the United States, but spent her time between the States and Sierra Leone, where her parents were from. At 18 years old, she chose to go to Sierra Leone to undergo female circumcision as part of her family's tribe's ritual; she chose to honor a tradition. To the Western feminist (the one that these theories rightly criticize), this might be confusing. How could Ahmadu—an educated, *westernized* woman—*choose* to undergo this mutilation? Well, her answer was one that theorist Njambi in the piece 'One Vagina to Go' explains as well: the western definition of "FGM" does not take into consideration many other forms of circumcision that not only do not take away pleasure for the woman but in fact give her a status boost and a more agentive role as a woman.

Sitting in the back of a University classroom for her lecture, staring at a slide of vaginas that detailed the four types of female circumcision—from least invasive (Ahmadu's tribe's custom) to most invasive (one defined as mutilation by Ahmadu)—I was confronted with my privilege. Again. I now cringe when I hear "Female Genital Mutilation" leaving the lips of a scholar who is hoping to change the world for African women everywhere by applying to the some "Third World" scholarship. Because, as Njambi so precisely words, this is another case of "reductive representations" of women in non-western cultures; another case of a group being firstly labeled a group and secondly defined as victims of a barbaric society.

The Vagina Monologues is a piece by Eve Ensler that is performed at many universities and other theater troops. When I first saw a version of it, I was floored by the candid nature of the monologues; the bluntness in language, the honesty in stories. In retrospect, however, I do see the sort of possessive nature and Marxist attitude some of these monologues can take in attempting to represent non-western women *for* them.

The monologues inadvertently created a hierarchy of expression and experience, one that encompasses Mohanty's term "Third World Difference." To "appropriate and colonize the fundamental complexities and conflicts which characterize the lives of women of different classes, religions, cultures, races, and castes in these countries" is to deny and erase the individual differences of each woman. So one vagina matters, and another does not; or rather a set of (western) vaginas matter in this particular way, and a set of (non-western) vaginas do not matter in that particular way. How do we deconstruct this?

Well, I particularly appreciate Mohanty's distinction between acts and modes, between the existence of a something and the context of that something when she said: "a woman's place is...not a product of the things she does...but the meaning her activities acquire through concrete social actions."

Here are my reactive questions to these theorists who get at the distinction between the ideological concept of "Woman," a majuscule W, versus the material subjects and stories about "women," with a lowercase W. Is the solution to hone in on the meaning society gives to these activities? How do we go about delineating this multitude of meanings across cultures? How can you *prove* universalism? If you can't, then how do we go about making tangible change? How do we recognize that our Western painting of women in developing countries is flawed, while also navigating that there are phenomena that exist in these countries that put us as part of the West in *highly privileged* positions?

After having seen and reflected on the Vagina Monologues as a whole, I find most problematic this approach of creating a "Woman," a whole idea and generalized discursive concept, that is ahistorical. We must historicize these women, their *individual* modes and intersections of oppression; but specifically both *before* and *after* their entry into social locations and relations as separate entities. My application of these ideas and theories continues to develop as I interact with women from all over the world. Recognizing my religious, racial, and cisgender privilege locates me as a *learner* when sitting across from a *tata* in a Senegalaise infant care home, versus sitting next to my Graphic Design friend who disclosed to me her choice of veiling and why. It is in these conversations that I see the problematic nature of the homogenization of a group; because that group is my neighbor or professor. Because that group is my friend.

So, I'd like to write a short letter about this concept of a global "sisterhood." This concept of all of us united at the feminist front:

Dear Western Feminist,

A few things to consider:

Firstly, I write to you because I was you, I am you. I am indeed from the West.

I don't mean to erase your individuality, but for the sake of this letter I must categorize you, just as you have categorized others.

You see, just because a woman is from the Middle East, does not mean she is battered or horribly controlled. Just because a woman chooses to veil because of her commitment to a religion does not mean she is a terrorist or that she is living in a restrictive society. And just because a culture is foreign to you, it does not make it okay to try to Westernize, or socially colonize, this culture.

Our mission as feminists is to elevate, not exploit. Women from around the world are not ours to *save*, as they have agency. Absolutely we should do what we can to help if we ever see a problem, but sometimes what we define as problematic—a veil, a religion, a government, a marriage—is exactly that: *our* opinion. The context of a woman cannot be essentialized by her continent: "all African women" "all women in the Middle East." Woman is a gender, a category; but there is not a universal gender experience. There is not a universal vagina.

Keep these things in your head when you engage with other women, other histories. And keep in mind that the West is not the center. We are not the center.

I hope I do not come off as patronizing, as I care about you which is why I am writing.

With love,

Abigail

Woman must have her freedom, the fundamental freedom of choosing whether or not she will be a mother and how many children she will have.

—MARGARET SANGER

* *

PART IV

Pale faced, I sip my apple juice. Well, that fucking hurt. My vagina had taken me to the doctor, yet again.

I had woken up at 8 AM, already a difficult obstacle for me, to go the Gynecologist. After November 8, 2016, I decided I would stop taking my orthrotricyclen and get an IUD; easy, right?

Intrauterine Device. Sounds medical, also kind of sounds like some sort of Artificial Implant for some intelligence company.

Anyway.

A friend of mine first mentioned the IUD when I was talking about the arm insert as a form of birth control.

"Yes, so I mean for women who have never given birth, it's supposed to really hurt. And it did, but for a split second."

Disclaimer: I have never given birth. But I thought, okay–our world is quickly becoming the Handmaid's Tale under the current administration, so I need to act fast.

I returned home from abroad, and made my appointment.

I went in wanting the copper IUD. No hormones, lasts on average 10 years I thought. Wait, first, you might not know what an IUD is.

According the the Planned Parenthood website:

"An IUD is a tiny device that's put into your uterus to prevent pregnancy. It's long-term, reversible, and one of the most effective birth control methods out there.

It's a small piece of flexible plastic shaped like a T.

There are 5 different brands of IUDs that are FDA approved for use in the United States: ParaGard, Mirena, Kyleena, Liletta, and Skyla.

These IUDs are divided into 2 types: copper IUDs (ParaGard) and hormonal IUDs (Mirena, Kyleena, Liletta, and Skyla)."

So I wanted the ParaGard; sounds kind of cool, yeah?

It's wrapped in copper that acts as a spermicide, and can last for up to 12 years. I went in ready. My gynecologist gave me the facts. The ParaGard is larger than the others, so it *really* hurts.

"How bad were your cramps before you started birth control?" she asked.

"I used to have to stay home from school." Yep, this is true. I remember by dad walking into my room once and I was curled into the fetal position and yelled "GET OUT DAD BLOOD IS COMING OUT OF MY VAGINA."

"Well, your cramps will look like that if you go non-hormonal. I would recommend the Kyleena. It uses the hormone progestin, and it works up to 5 years."

Okay, settled.

I changed into a robe, and I waited.

My gynecologist comes in, she's being really supportive. She's all about letting me know the pain will be so temporary, and that so many women do this daily that I'll be okay.

I take a deep breath. I think of my sister. She recently turned

33. When her birthday rolls around, I like to send her a happy 50th birthday text because we joke that she's too old. But really, she's not. And, moreover, she's one of the strongest women I have had the pleasure of knowing.

Her first daughter, Grace, was born February 25, 2014. Lauralee did not choose to use any narcotics during labor. I held her baby and cried silently; a beautiful child, made from my sister.

Her second daughter, Noelle, was born August 2, 2016. Again, Lauralee took on childbirth like it was her job. It kind of was, in the moment at least.

So when I was screaming profanity and incredibly uncomfortable, enduring a shooting pain I could not quite place because the IUD induces contractions—i.e. my cervix was dilating—I thought of Lauralee. When I was, as the nurse told me, pale as a ghost after a two minute procedure, I thought of Lauralee. She did that for *hours*, as many women do if they choose *and* are able to have a child vaginally.

As I sipped on my apple juice like a child, still at the Gynecologist after about 45 minutes, I thought of Lauralee. I remember seeing her after she delivered Grace. She was beautiful, she was a fortress.

She used to drive me to school when I was in Kindergarten; she was a senior. I only have one faint memory of her at the wheel. It's not even really a memory, more a brief image; but it has remained in my head since that day. She was the second mother of our family. She left to go to college when I was little, so while we didn't necessarily grow up together, she forged a path that I could follow. One of vocal opinions, of loyalty, and one of getting shit done. Because, without fail, that's what she does. No questions.

And that's what she did when she had those beautiful girls.

So as I finished my apple juice, changed out of my robe, and contemplated the T-shape plastic device in my uterus, I thanked her in my head.

CHAPTER 5

———

There is no such thing as a single-issue struggle because we do not live single-issue lives.

—AUDRE LORDE

PART I

I signed up for Queer Theory to, honestly, spite my parents. My upbringing was very white, very straight, and very middle-upper class. Queer Theory introduced me to a world I had no idea I was missing, and have since plunged into with pride.

I first learned the word heteronormative sitting across from Jacob Brogan, my professor of this class, and I thought "holy shit I've been living this stuff my *entire* life." The "this" was a social construction that the normal is straight, the normal is middle class, and, to be frank, that the normal is white. This construction was never explicitly verbalized, but it existed in the form of mid-calve Nike socks, student's disappointment in Obama's 2008 victory, and the usage of "faggot" as a synonym for lame.

At the end of my semester, I approached my professor with my two favorite excerpts from the class.

"What should I take if these essays were what resonated?" For some reason I was nervous approaching this mind that had given my path the coolest 180.

"You should check out Intro to Sexuality Studies. It's a Women's and Gender Studies course."

This is where I will quickly say thank you, Jacob Brogan, for changing my life.

* *

Talk to her about sex, and start early. It will probably be a bit awkward, but it is necessary.

—CHIMAMANDA NGOZI ADICHIE

* *

PART II

Every time Michelle Ohnona speaks, I am more and more in awe of her intellect. When I first walked into her classroom, I was overwhelmed by the tall people. They were clearly seniors, and I, the lowly, ignorant freshman; but she did not see it this way. Foucault became a friend, *The Mask You Live In* a frequent tear jerker, heteronormativity a quotidian word.

Years after having taken her Intro to Sexuality Studies course, I spoke with Ohnona on the phone while sitting at my desk job.

Total radio silence. This was sexual education for Michelle Ohnona from grades 7 to 12.

Ohnona, now a professor of Sexuality Studies and Women's and Gender Studies at Georgetown University, said her interest in sexuality studies emerged even before her experience as an undergraduate. Growing up in Montréal, her mother encouraged the pursuit of information when it came to sex and relationships; consequently Ohnona quickly became the high school "doctor" of sorts.

Picture HelloFlo, the company that sends period products right to your door. My favorite of their commercials, "The Camp Gyno," stars a pubescent camper as narrator who is the first to have her period, or, what she deems the "red badge of courage." As the "Joan of Arc" of periods, the narrator deals tampons, uses dolls and ketchup for demonstrations, and coaches campers through their cramps.

This was Ohnona. She was thrust into a role of sexual educator; and when a female peer asked her if you can get HIV/AIDS from kissing, 10th grade Ohnona approached the principal of the school demanding for *some* sort of sexual education. Following her query, the principal set up a singular info session in which the teacher left the room and Ohnona asked her fellow classmates what questions they had. The purpose was to demonstrate to the administration that many of the girls were sexually active but felt really uninformed; not only about issues about pregnancy and contraception but also consent. For an all girls Catholic high school, Ohnona was disturbed by the lack of access to information, especially given that the vast majority of her teachers were women; she felt as if they had an obligation to step up for their students and provide the guidance these girls were so desperately seeking. It was as if the school was gambling with the well being of their students, because the Camp Gyno does not always have the right answers.

So if you have 16 year old Anita, who can identify the vulva and confide in her sex ed teacher, next to a 16 year old student from Ohnona's school, who believes there could be a link between kissing and STIs, you can understand why Sexuality Studies at the University level can be complicated. This is what

Ohnona deems an "unevenness in student experience," as you have freshman whose high school promoted Gay/Straight alliance groups partnering with students who have never discussed sexuality in the context of integrity. The different strata of fluency among undergraduates when it comes to activism and sexual education pose a challenge for college educators like Ohnona, whose goal is to meet *every* student at their individual level.

The issue comes when dominant voices in these classrooms, whether physically or through body language, begin to exclude other voices. Ohnona described a year where a group of bright and committed students who identified as queer thought themselves to be the only queer voices in the room, and consequently diminished closeted voices without knowing. This is where damage can occur; and it is the fault of the pre-University sexual education system that disadvantages the progressive thinking of students and perhaps harms their ability to vocalize their own identity.

From my desk job to Poulton Hall (an under-the-radar building for most Georgetown freshmen, and other members of the student body for that matter), I spoke to Jennifer Wiggins, a Staff Clinician and Sexual Assault Specialist, Rape Crisis counselor. She described her role as three pronged: Education, Clinical, Advocacy. All intersect and manifest as a SAPE

(Sexual Assault Peer Educators) curriculum, emotional support, and a focus on Title IX issues, to sum up an incredibly difficult job in one sentence.

"I had never been exposed to sexual assault in a very formal way until grad school. I went to a small, private, catholic institution. . . but no one ever used the term sexual assault."

Wiggins knew she wanted to do community health work, but at 21 was unsure what that actually meant in the real world. She chose to take a trauma course about sexual assault that took place half the time in the classroom, and the other half in a rape crisis center in Philly.

"The youngest person I helped was 3 and the oldest person was in her late 80s." My stomach drops. This is her *job*. Needless to say, Wiggins came into her new job with experience whose depth was simply unknown by many others.

"We meet students where they are. Students might come every day when they're in crisis. Clinically it can vary depending upon their person and their needs."

And each background of the individual shifts the lens with which they view the world, sex, and their relationship to both of these components. Any marginalized identity is at a greater risk of perpetration. Black women are three time more likely than white women to be sexually assaulted; indigenous women five times more likely. Gender non-conforming/queer students are also at a greater disadvantage.

"These communities have nuances that either encourage or discourage them from engaging in conversations about sexual violence."

For example, perhaps certain queer students have these conversations slightly more easily in their spaces, at an intersection of white privilege and sexual orientation, described Wiggins. Students of color, however, live in a different unfair space that our society has constructed. For many of these students, violence sometimes gets normalized because a majority of systems do not support racial identities in ways that feel safe and comfortable. So when faced with two layers of oppression, many students of color are forced to fight for their more salient identity regarding race versus survivorship—how can a 21 year old be expected to prioritize facing a society that has constructed this notion of race and gender and all things in between and tangential?

Within conversations across demographics, Wiggins always comes across the difficult discussion about consent:

If you look at the more impactful sex education programs, there's this whole piece where we're actually talking about sex and how to engage in it. Here we talk about consent but we don't have the ability to talk about sex because we are a catholic jesuit institutional context...

...So what we do is talk *around* consent...we can talk about it in a counseling space but...we skip a couple steps because I can talk to you about consent but if I can't even have a conversation with you about how to even like engage in the conversation around sex how can we talk about consent...

...People are like 'consent is very gray' and I'm like 'mmm it's more black and white,' but it's really hard to equal the playing field.

If sex itself is taboo, than the attempt to conceptualize consent in a concrete way becomes incredibly difficult.

"We have a tendency to dissect [sex] as a philosophy."

When it comes to oneself and one's experiences, we are not equipped to understand where the line of academia and theories ends and our personal safety and well being begins. But this is where the Venn Diagram of education on consent and actions of others turns into images of violence.

CHAPTER 6

PART I

OCTOBER 17, 2017

*When I was groped by a classmate in science class at age 12,
I didn't say anything, feeling ashamed. When a PE teacher
pressed his entire body against the back of mine at age 13, I
didn't say anything, except later to friends—two of whom
revealed that he'd done the same to them.*

Laurie Berger, designer on the creative team at Pinterest, wrote
these words.

We were at a bar in Lyon, France, during our semester abroad.
I was 20 at the time. My friends and I had decided to explore

the city through bar hopping, a way to connect with the young *français* and mess around. A man approached me, and in French, "complimented" my chest. Perhaps he thought I wouldn't understand, or assumed I would take it as an actual compliment, but my friend chuckled knowing that this man had just chosen the wrong girl at the bar. I whipped around, and proceeded to give him my opinion in words he could understand; French that is. He stood there, and paused. Seeing my friend Will next to me, he thought the best response would be to apologize, as he didn't realize I had a boyfriend. Aah, yes; because it would have been okay otherwise. I informed him that this was my friend, not boyfriend, and that a piece of information such as my relationship status does not merit an apology, but instead that the piece of information that is me being a human merited the apology.

Laurie finished her Facebook post:

> I don't know why I often can't find words to express myself to the perpetrator in the moment. I suppose I'm scared, afraid of escalating the offense to something more scarring, especially when I'm alone. But I think about these occurrences long after they're over and I'm so, so grateful to those who stand up for themselves and and others and communicate that this is not okay. Keep doing it, and next time this happens, I will too.

Thank you Laurie, I will too.

Stories like this are the reason that, if you've been in the University system recently, your first day of college orientation has a sexual violence training, or a quiz online due by the end of September where you pick which scenario is the safest. Sexual violence and/or harassment occurs often, and disproportionately affects women. Whether it's the Mad Men style boss-secretary scenario, or the wild statistics of college women assaulted compared to men.

Laurie's words above are just a prerequisite to understanding the gravity of why these trainings exist. It normally takes the form of a sketch, or SIM-like computer clips where you choose the serving size for each type of alcohol or how Susan should get out of a tricky situation. How did we get here, then?

In 1994, Congress passed the Violence Against Women Act (VAWA), drafted originally by the office of former Vice President Joe Biden, then serving as the Senator of Delaware. The act was a product of contributors from various fields— including but not limited to psychology, health and wellness, advocacy, and survivorship; because sexual violence is not restricted to one domain nor does it have just one consequence. It's a compilation piece.

"We have to take [rape culture] on wherever we find it in our society, whether it's the so-called locker room talk, or bar banter, or the tasteless joke—anything that condones or even promotes violence against women," Biden, explained.

The snippet above comes from an interview Biden conducted this past January with Refinery29. From 1994 to now, we have been able to name a violence that is specific—sexual violence—and continue to take proactive steps to deconstruct it and its perpetrators.

The original goal of the act was to reframe the ways in which law enforcement approaches sexual assault and domestic violence, and its evolution lead to reforms and campaigns all in the name of prevention education. From 1993 to 2014, the rate of domestic violence in the United States dropped by 72%.

Biden's badasserie does not change the fact that 1 in 5 woman are sexually assaulted before they leave college, compared to 1 in 20 men. Do the math. That means women are four times more likely to be victims of sexual assault; and that is white women. Women of color, Native American women, and Hispanic women's statistics are even more wince-inducing. And those are the numbers of people who are *reporting* their assault. Many others remain silent. From these interactions emerge two narratives—that of the perpetrator and the victim—that pointedly highlight the disparity of gender in this country.

Back with Jennifer Wiggins in Poulton Hall, I asked about the ways in which this disparity takes form within the context of sexual assault, specifically with college students.

"So then in a college space," says Wiggins, "I think we have this interesting concept of ruining a perpetrator's life and it makes me think of Brock Turner." If that name doesn't ring a bell, perhaps "Stanford Swimmer" will. In the case of People v. Turner back in 2016, Brock Turner was accused—with two witnesses on the scene—to have raped an unconscious woman behind a dumpster after a college party. At the time, Turner was a student athlete at Stanford University, hence the nickname. Even after two witnesses who testified, and given the fact that Turner fled the scene when confronted by said witnesses, Turner received 6 months of a sentence with three years of probation. How is it that this young boy, whose picture used in response to his allegations was his *school* photo (rather than his mug shot), gets off on a very light charge in the era of mass incarceration we are living right now? We do not understand consent, so we go with what we know: language that excuses white men in particular and that silences the victim. We construct sexual assault and harassment as mistakes, but, as Wiggins so pointedly stated, "we don't use that theory for any [other] type of crime." My jaw dropped. When it comes to mass incarceration, we are ready to dispose of bodies of color or underline a one time crime or even a small pattern of crime as *needing* to determine the rest of the person's life; but when it comes to sexual assault, we reduce it to a heteronormative issue about sex, wealth, and power. The social capital that those with wealth have built around their identities becomes an un-penetrable barrier.

What does this lead to?

I went to go see a brilliant play called *Infinite Wrench* back in the fall. The play was composed of, if I remember correctly, 30 mini plays that had one hour to be carried out. They were student written, based on real experience, and each took on a new and intriguing format.

A friend of mine stood on stage with a white board and a hangman game outlined. It read:

$$\_\_ \cdot _____\text{'}_____ \textit{got into}$$
Georgetown Law.

The audience screamed out letters, getting excited to participate and influence the actors on stage. The end result silenced the audience. I felt a tear escape my eye.

MY BEST FRIEND'S RAPIST got into Georgetown Law.

That is what these un-penetrable fortresses lead to. A perpetrator in your classroom, and, in the words of Wiggins, "a president who can go on tape and basically admit he is a perpetrator and can still be our president."

There is an unfortunate and yet ingrained habit of policing the bodies of other people through sexual violence and language.

Wiggins introduced me to the Pyramid of Sexual Violence:

THE BASE: attitudes and beliefs such as racism, sexism, ableism, homophobia.

THE MIDDLE: verbal expression, such as sexual harassment, sexual jokes, bragging.

THE PEAK: Physical expression, sexual assault.

"When people green light these things, they only have the tendency to grow."

I guess the light is green. I hope for the sake of many bodies and histories, it turns red eventually.

PART II

In 2011, Biden introduced a new set of guidelines whose objective, much like the VAWA, was to improve the ways in which we confront sexual violence but this time on college campuses specifically. The two main objectives goals were as follows, according to a CBS news cover:

- To provide educators with the tools to better understand and prevent sexual assault on campus
- And to "clarify the legal obligations of schools receiving federal funding under Title IX—which prohibits discrimination in education programs and activities on the basis of gender—in regard to responding to incidents of sexual assault or violence."

The It's On Us movement came about in September of 2014 as yet another proactive step in combatting harmful sexual violence statistics.

Biden, again, outlined the social movement's focus: "student-centered movement that engages all aspects of campuses from the presidents, to the football coaches, to the fraternities, to student activists, and everyone in the middle to push the message that everyone has an obligation to step up, step in, and stop sexual assaults."

The It's On Us website is a playground of statistics and awareness when it comes to gendered sexual violence. The idea is to take apart the rape schema we have engrained in our minds. For instance, 9 in 10 women who are undergraduate students and victims of rape and sexual violence *know* the perpetrator personally. One of them is named Emma Sulkowitz.

MAY 17, 2015

Emma Sulkowitz graduated from Columbia University.

I heard Emma's story for the first time when visiting a Virginia private University, when a student spotted the symbol on the underside of my right wrist.

"Badass. That tattoo is badass."

"This one? Well thanks. I got it last fall when I was studying abroad in Lyon, France. I was wandering the streets of Croix-Rousse, this sort of hipster-y neighborhood, with a friend of mine. We had entertained the ideas of tattoos, so when we passed a parlor we went for it."

"Duuude did it hurt?"

"Honestly no, it lasted about 10 minutes. It probably hurt my bank account more—80 euro for this small Venus symbol. But honestly it was so worth it. I have four sisters, a baller mom, and I'm a Women's and Gender Studies major so it just seemed fitting."

"Women's and Gender Studies?? Wow, do you go here? You're one of the few seemingly liberals I've run into. . . . You'd DIE over my thesis. I'm writing it about Emma Sulkowitz."

"Hmm I recognize that name, who is she again?"

Emma Sulkowitz spent her senior year carrying her dorm mattress all over campus—including her college graduation from Columbia University—on her back. Because you see Emma Sulkowitz was raped in her dorm at Columbia in 2012, and the perpetrator had not been expelled or suspended. The following is an excerpt from *TIME,* published in May 2014, a year before Sulkowitz's graduation and mattress project:

> I was raped by a fellow classmate the first day of my sophomore year. I didn't report it at first because I didn't feel like dealing with the emotional trauma. But then I met two other women who told me the same person who had assaulted me assaulted them, and I decided I had to do something. We all reported our cases, and all three were dismissed.

Think back to your sophomore year of college (or forward, if you're not there yet). Sophomore year is weird. You no longer have to look up how to get to your Psych class building, but you still have a fake ID and eat Kraft Mac and Cheese for dinner. If you're me, you live on the lower bunk bed with your roommate from last year surrounded by puke green carpet and the echoes of outdoor construction. Amidst the chaos that is the edge of 19 and the transition to 20, many find themselves in their safest mindset in bed, in their dorm room or apartment. Now imagine if that space—mine covered with twinkly white lights and goofy pictures of my friends and family—was invaded. This was Emma's story. Her mattress had gone from a place of security to a place of paralysis. Her twinkly white lights were a signal of peril; her goofy thumbtacked pictures were a reminder of fear. And what's worse, Emma had to open up her bedroom doors, uncover her mattress, and break any wall of intimacy and privacy down in order to have her story be told.

> During my hearing, which didn't take place until seven months after the incident, one panelist kept asking me how it was physically possible for anal rape to happen. I was put in the horrible position of trying to educate her and explain how this terrible thing happened to me.

Emma's experience is not an anomaly. Her story mirrors that of Anita Hill, who in 1991 testified against Judge Clarence Thomas who she argues sexually harrassed her while she worked under him; in a room of white, older men, Hill was required to detail almost every sexual act of which she accused Thomas, including how he would measure the length of his penis in front of her. Her story reflects that of Ashley Judd, who was lured into Harvey Weinstein's hotel room and asked to massage him naked or watch him shower. Her story flies me back to my semester abroad.

I was visiting Strasbourg with a tour group last fall during my study abroad program in Lyon, France. It was late November or early December—I remember because it was Christmas Season so Strasbourg's Christmas Markets were our target. Myself and three other close girl friends from Lyon got on a group bus at 5 A.M. on Saturday in order to embark on a 24 hour trip to see these markets and try hot wine. Our welcoming committee in this French/German town was a not-so-warm-and-fuzzy hostel staff. After a few (inefficient) hours of waiting and organizing, we were each assigned different bedrooms; I was placed in a bedroom with four strangers that all happened to be men. When I asked if I could perhaps switch or change rooms to be with my friends, the program leaders seemed stuck; apparently, this was a hard ask. I forgot about it, placed my things in the room, and my friends and I went into town to explore. That night, I had my friend Sophie sleep with me in a twin bed as a precaution. As we heard four pairs of clamorous legs coming down the hallway, we thought it best to pretend to be asleep in order to avoid unnecessary conversation blurred by their drunken stupor. Bursting into the door, an English accent exclaimed, "Who is the random girl staying in here again? We should totally gang-bang her." Yes, that is what I heard while in a small, foreign town across the ocean from my home.

These stories are both common and outrageously disturbing. In fact, I would guess you may want to put this book down because of a poor taste in your mouth or tight knot in your stomach; but I urge you not to. Rape is a word that makes us cringe, as it should, but its meaning has somehow gotten lost along the way. Rape is not something that only happens to the girl coming home late at night, dragged to an alleyway by a stranger in a dark mask. Sexual harassment is not something that only occurs when on the subway by an unfamiliar face. Crude phrases like "gang-bang" and "fucking that bitch" are not only in R-rated movies where the bad guys are discussing their escapades. These actions, these words, these stories happen *everywhere* with *anyone*—not excluding your best friend, or the guy who sits next to you in finance class, or the person whose cubicle touches yours, or your partner. Our education, our society, and our media have all handed us a misguided rape schema; so that when we are taken aback by the word "whore" escaping our partner's lips or "bitch" following your high school classmate's laugh or a slap on our backside by our boss, we do not know how to respond.

Emma Sulkowitz spent her senior year carrying her dorm mattress all over campus. She became a symbol for women everywhere, much like the Venus tattoo on my wrist.

Two years later, and the trending hashtag and movement, #MeToo, evolved as a powerful symbol in reaction to the domino effect of Harvey Weinstein allegations this past Fall. In 2006, Tarana Burke created the famous slogan to raise awareness of sexual violence and survivorship; a little over a decade later actress Alyssa Milano posted the powerful phrase in the following tweet:

"Suggested by a friend: If all the women who have been sexually harassed or assaulted wrote "Me too" as a status, we might give people a sense of the magnitude of the problem." (Or, if you're French, the brilliant hashtag is #balancetonporc, squeal on your pig).

That black backdrop, three upside-down triangles that go from white, to gray, to black. It's the beginning of so many movies we have all seen. The Weinstein Company stares back in bright white. Once a symbol of cinematic genius; it now serves as a reminder of an abuse of power.

I first heard of the Harvey Weinstein allegations after my French class this past fall. My friends and I were crowded around our living room table, listening to a recording of Ambra Battilana Gutierrez, an Italian Model who had recorded Weinstein with a police wire in 2015 in an effort to get him to confess his misconduct.

His voice was chilling; and not in an ASMR before bed kind of way. He sounded frantic. In so many words, he kept telling

Gutierrez to be quiet and that he was famous so if she went with him it'd be okay. We had been celebrating Rosh Hashanah for one of my roommates; by the end of the dinner we all had stomach aches, and they were not from our meal.

The media's reaction unfolded in a Timeline that is still unfolding. The names are endless: Rose McGowan, Ashley Judd, Romola Garai, Gwyneth Paltrow, Angelina Jolie, 13 anonymous women via a piece in the New Yorker...the list goes on and on. A history of hotel room stories, naked massages, shower invitations—all using a position to manipulate those Weinstein viewed as inferior and vulnerable. Sex as a power tool, a weapon. In these cases, the women above at least had an eventual moment to speak out. One of their intersectional pieces—race and economic status for example—provided *some* sort of platform, no matter how debatably faulty given the power of the man they were up against. Others remain silenced; because unfortunately, sex as a weapon of violence, and power catalyzed by a patriarchal structure to oppress those more vulnerable, is not always in the light of the media. Many a time, it hides in the shadows.

PART III

The following is a story I struggle with, as it is personal and off-putting; but it is important to share. So as I sit here to wrap up this chapter, I am taking a deep breath. Please note that I have left out the names and some details that could be construed as graphic in the below story in order to maintain the anonymity of those involved and protect those reading; well, besides me.

I was in college. It was a celebratory night with friends, and we were all out hastily excited to attend a fun happy hour. A friend of mine and I were catching up, and we were not necessarily being the most responsible with our alcohol intake. He whispers something to me that confuses me, and then runs out of the bar. After I drunkenly follow him, the memory is quite hazy; but the rest was not one that I happily recount.

I remember being pinned down. He was heavier than me so it was harder to navigate. This was someone I was close to, so I was surprised. It was quick. It wasn't painful or anything, so I told myself it was fine. He left immediately.

It's hard to move past a moment like that. It's hard when you regret something and can't tell what really was happening. Sex is a weapon, a strategy, a tool. And sometimes a close friend, without even conceptualizing how you might react to the event, uses that tool to (in my case) his advantage. I went back and forth when deciding whether or not I include this story that makes me even more vulnerable than I thought I could be throughout this book. My final reason for including this is because it makes the above stories—ones that are perhaps more distant, more public—tangible and more real. It shows my direct relationship with this chapter, and will maybe encourage you to consider those in your life who have experienced something to this extent. Because the unfortunate fact is that there are many of us. But that's why we fight.

CHAPTER 7

———

"I really loved Washington, DC, so I kept coming back here."

Sitting in my sister's bedroom in Gaithersburg, Maryland, I am on the phone with Sasanka Jinadasa, a Harvard graduate and my former supervisor at HIPS. She was a half-shaved head, badass figure that my eyes followed in the office thinking "damn, I want to creatively lead as she does."

I asked Jinadasa to expand upon what HIPS does, what it is, and why she stuck with it:

> HIPS is a organization, a harm reduction organization, for people who trade sex and use drugs, speaking to their individual power and agency; and I think why what HIPS does is so important. It truly when done right and done

well and on mission...it is really about making sure that it's in somebody's power to make the most accessible choice that HIPS can provide to them. HIPS will do everything they can to give you as many options as possible; which is something society works so hard to do for many groups of people...

...I wanted to be part of an organization that understood what intersectionality was. And how those intersections fundamentally transform people's social locations and access. The local work was so phenomenally important, and I got involved because of my community because I am a person of color. And I stayed because of my community.

As for me, I first entered the HIPS space at age 20, in a suit for an interview. I was the odd one out. A white chick in a brown Zara suit walks into a harm reduction clinic....

I sat in a sunken, comfily ripped couch. The woman across from me had a presence. I will keep her name anonymous, but she would later become a friend of mine. She was funny, sassy, and had a story of a warrior. A trans woman of color who attended Howard, traded sex and drugs, and was a teacher just as much as she was my friend.

Back in Gaithersburg, I ask Jinadasa about her career as an advocate and activist:

Well, I was a Social Media fellow at the US Conference on AIDS. I approached the keynote speaker, and asked, 'what keeps you going?' essentially.

'Well what's the alternative?' And I guess that's it. We do the work because we have to. Because once you see injustice it becomes very hard to unsee. It's like, well, have you seen the Matrix? When you take the pill in the Matrix and they're like 'oh shit.' Basically the same thing. We figure out ways to sustain ourselves and each other. What is the alternative? Just. . . let injustice happen? That's not acceptable.

When listening to the recording of our interview you hear, after her response and the recording goes silent; then you hear me. "Woah. Well, damn." Because that's how I felt. . . damn.

My first day at HIPS was a wake up call. On the second floor of the clinic, the interns sat around a large round table taking up a majority of the conference room's space. Some of the interns had previous experience with Harm Reduction and sex work, so our first few days of training were a simple review. For me, I was completely in the dark. I thought 'okay, I've got the empathy card, I can do this.' But I don't think I realized the extent to which my engrained values, both conscious and subconscious, would be challenged and stretched like a rubber band ball.

That first day, Jinadasa walked in with a penis structure; if I recall, it was blue, not a tan "skin" color.

"Does anyone know how to put a condom on with their mouths?"

Needless to say, I learned. I called my mom that evening to recount the story for shock value.

"Hmm so why exactly did you need to learn that trick?" she asked.

Well, it's because many sex workers would like to have protective sex, but their clients refuse. So they learn how to maneuver their clients' desires while also making the safest decision for themselves. As someone who had never been exposed to sex workers—other than the dramatized "prostitutes" in films and watering mouths talking about the red light district in Amsterdam—I had never quite internalized this concept of protecting oneself in the midst of a sexual transaction.

My mind had wandered—I went back to Jinadasa on the phone.

"Let's talk about the stigma around sex work." This is my transition "question" for her.

"I think we see it all the time," she started. "I was talking to a friend of mine who is an attorney this morning about...[the future and the policy] if we considered sex work to be work...but there's a way that we put sex on a certain type of pedestal where we make sex, 'sex with the right person'...[but] all of these models around sex are so difficult to access."

She continued with a Foucault styled narrative on power and pleasure that stung me, in a good way.

We have made sex, she says, "a form of pleasure incomparable to other forms of pleasure...[and] also when it's violent it's uniquely violent. So there's a way that sex has been given power, and people seek to disempower this imbalance."

There exists a dichotomy surrounding sex, because, you know, binaries are everywhere.

A BRIEF BACKGROUND ON BINARIES (A SIDE NOTE):

Binaries are concepts that exist as the composition of two things. For example, black and white; peanut butter and jelly. In many cases, and more often than not in our society and historically, gender is presented as a binary: man and/or woman. Once you take note of a binary, you start to notice them all; moreover, you start to notice how they can be dangerous. In a society that prides itself on binaries, those who do not fit into that narrative (asexual, non gender conforming, and/or queer individuals, for example) become marginalized.

A binary that has recently deeply affected me is one of "inside/outside;" that is, those who are incarcerated and those who walk free.

I recently have been visiting the DC Jail as part of work with the Prisons and Justice Initiative. After only two weeks of visiting, I consider many of those inside my friends. I am in the midst of writing letters to them, and to creating sustainable relationships for once they get out, if they are on track to that is. It hits me when I leave that I get to go outside, be outside; and they do not. I walk free; they are walked by guards. In the education room, the library where we all sit and conduct a class, I hear them speak to their experience and their minds unfold before me. They are brilliant, incredibly well-read; they are kind. My eyes fill up with tears. Society has demonized them, has taken them away from the sidewalks and caged them like animals. Binaries do not just affect your lunch (back to the peanut butter and jelly example). They affect people's lives permanently.

This story, my friends, serve as an example of the ways in which binaries distort reality and create false categories around all sorts of fluid categories. The main message from this side note: binaries are deceptive.

* *

Gender equality is more than a goal in itself. It is a precondition for meeting the challenge of reducing poverty, promoting sustainable development and building good governance.

—KOFI ANNAN

* *

Okay, now back to Jinadasa, and the binary of sex as an act.

You have: "let's banish sex, that's how we're going to disempower. [it]," she said.

And then there's: "everybody have sex. . .and have it everywhere. . .and that's how we disempower it."

Jinadasa continued to paint images of this question that I was racing to type:

> It's probably more complex than that, this sort of mystical power sex has and the hold it has societally. I think there is a value to listening to each other and talking to each other and not pathologizing it or medicalizing it but starting to listen to feelings people have around sex. I mean that would be a great way. . .to start to remove criminal

legal systems' [attitudes around] sex... when we're talking about sexual violence to focus on the violence part as opposed to sex part. But then again, just because you ignore something's power doesn't mean it doesn't have it. We give sex power and then we're afraid of it.

She had just woven the web between socialization, criminalization, sex, violence, power, race, and gender all in one bulk quote on this page. I reflected on the scenario we were taught in HIPS training.

If a woman is raped while with a client—because that is *more* than possible and, in fact, occurs often—she cannot report this to the police without being placed *herself* in jail. Because the work she has done—to feed her children, to pay her rent, or just because this is the career she finds most lucrative and enjoys—is illegal.

So how do we encourage people to educate themselves and advocate, I asked.

I would just want people to start thinking beyond themselves... that's the initial starting point, how do you develop a plethora of perspectives and an internal analysis. Often when people start to think about that... about 'how do I advocate by and for people in a way that involves those values'... [there are answers]. People need to do a lot of self-investment...rather than a couple community service hours.

At that's what HIPS allows for its clients and its employees, and its Georgetown bubbled interns like me.

I think there's a way that working at HIPS showed me how much...this is something I think about a lot...what's most important is knowing what you don't know and trusting people with experience. I might not make the choices someone else made...but I only think that's because I don't know their life. Two people could make two completely different and both completely valid choices as to how to live their lives.

HIPS seeks to show the choices that exist, for the marginalized communities seeking them.

I continue, "so what is the mission exactly? What is the goal?"

Society works really hard to make sure the straight, able-bodied, white man has as many options as possible, HIPS just believes that equitably, the same things should be true for everyone else. And whether that's like you should have access to a great clinic, you should have access to...um...great housing, you should have access to health like you should just have it. It's so holistic and that's what's important about it. The mission is to improve the quality of life for people who trade sex and use drugs. . . like to make sure that every sex worker knows their status. . . which is a great goal.

This playing field we always talk about equaling, Jinadasa works to actually do that, for everyone. And it started at Harvard.

Harvard, it's not geared towards progress. . . and I mean I had friends who were doing much cooler work at Harvard than I ever did. It was not super conducive to getting progressive stuff done, but it was such a great training ground to think about pushing people who don't want to be pushed. And then I also met a bunch of brilliant people who were really incredible activists; and I also had amazing professors. . .

. . . It was mostly administration that you had to push-back against the most..and people say that the University is what turns out activists. . . and that's probably [because] we don't give resources to people that are on the ground. . .

. . . One of the people I know at HIPS who had been to prison was like 'prison was the first place that I got to sit down and think.' And i was like that's really fucked up that i got to live a life where I went to University where like that was sort of what my job was. One of my jobs was to think..and to reflect and to learn. And I think that's also something that like University students should take advantage of and really think about is that you're in a place where some people literally in the world are navigating survival so hard. . .and they never ever in their life get a chance to just think. And it's something that I think students in University should value. I don't think I valued it enough in college. What an absolute privilege it is to just be able to slow down your life and just think.

For Jinadasa, Harvard catalyzed a world of activism and awareness. For me, my Intro to Women's and Gender Studies professor's recommendation to look up the HIPS website catalyzed mine. HIPS provided me with a toolbox I never saw coming. So when I found myself on a weekend trip to Amsterdam while abroad, I peppered my tour guide Bas with questions rooted in harm reduction and legalized sex work for the entirety of the three hour traverse of the city.

Posted across the Red Light District neighborhood in Amsterdam multiple signs read "Please, No Photos While Women are Working." After 3 months on 9th and H, trying desperately to fight for some sort of mere recognition of sex workers' rights and their status as *workers*—even amongst many in my political circle—the sign felt like a weight lifted off of my shoulders. Because a place where sex work is regulated and protected further validates the women within these fields; and the fact of the matter is this field will most likely continue to exist for a long time, if not indefinitely. Being in an area that does not judge those who choose to be involved in sex work felt liberating. It was the HIPS building expanded across an entire city. A history of vulnerability and empathy entrenched in the upbringing of a culture made me hopeful.

Yes, sex will always hold some sort of power in our lives, be it religious, political, gendered, or otherwise; but a step of acknowledgement of how to denounce its harmful power— via a sign or a clinic or a conversation—is a valid step indeed.

CHAPTER 8

When we stick together as women, as girls, as sisters, we can achieve the extraordinary.

—JANELLE MONAE

Choice in three parts.

PART I

I watch Family Feud with my grandmother when I'm home. It's something the two of us can spend time doing that doesn't end in political frustration around Fox News or my "liberal brain washing."

Last week, while home for Thanksgiving, Steve Harvey read

the question: "what is something that men can do in public that women would be told was inappropriate?"

Fight, burp, and other random acts were guessed. The number one answer? Be shirtless.

This is a topic on which I have no *visceral* opinion, but I think exploring it is incredibly important. Once reframed in terms of a conversation about choice, well then I certainly have something to say.

"We live in a world where we're obsessed with women's breast... but the nipple is hidden." Actress and activist Lino Esco had a film idea to play with an androcentric audience, and unite women under a common goal: to pushback against a tradition regarding women's bodies. From here, her idea became the Free the Nipple movement.

"I wanted women to go topless in NYC to challenge the censorship laws for equality." The result? "The nipple has been hidden for so long... that now that it's just peeking out for a minute people are freaking out."

I thought of the bold women strutting through Manhattan to make a statement. This act goes beyond a radical reflection of the body, no matter how powerful the manifest may be, and uses a body in a way that was *chosen*. The women *chose* to do the uncomfortable, and get in people's faces. I question the uproar that followed this movement; because yes, it is unconventional, and perhaps would confuse the white suburban family walking by. But we see women's bodies all the time. They are the cover of a billboard to get you to buy insurance, or the protagonist of a beer commercial, or your waitress at a late night restaurant. So we sell their bodies—commercially and/or physically—but we do not allow women to simply *wear* their naked bodies. Because we inevitably sexualize women's bodies as a society.

According to Esco, "there are no healthy images of women being topless," so she took an opportunity and created that healthy image. This goes back to abortion, menstruation, working while parenting, and any gendered topic where the choice of the woman is ignored. We glorify a male gaze, one that follows the curves of her figure, but we do not respect the female desire or decision. We strip her of her agency in order to please an androcentric, heteronormative, white audience.

While watching Family Feud, my mind raced through the outline of this chapter I could create. And at the same time, the audience on the Game Show Network just laughed.

* *

I myself have never been able to find out precisely what feminism is: I only know that people call me a feminist whenever I express sentiments that differentiate me from a doormat.

—REBECCA WEST

* *

PART II

Professor Sara Collina found feminism when she started at Cornell, "and it was like a religion." It was an outlet of empowerment not just because of its content, but because Collina, who now teaches Gender and the Law at Georgetown University, discovered creativity and became an expert within a field; a professional empowerment that was not confined to classroom walls.

But there still existed dichotomies within feminism and Collina's education that she could not quite navigate. In high school, she hoped for a future featuring a baby, but it was not the "cool feminist thing to do." It provoked images of 1950s housewives, an image that many progressive feminists in both Collina's and my time denounce. I remember my freshman year here at Georgetown, I was scanning through GroupMe and my stomach cramped upon reading a post from an older girl who worked with me. It was something along the lines of how she wanted to be a mom, but "not a stay-at-home mom because #feminism." I was livid. My mother had raised five women whose goals and paths intertwined and deviated as an art form. After her second child, not having anticipated the difficulty of finding a balance between being a journalist and raising daughters, she chose to stay at home. While I am certainly biased, I'd say her decision changed the lives of five women, one of them being me. I would not be writing these words had I not had my mom by my side when I did; and while there may be seeds of regret or questions sprinkled in all of our lives, the question of whether my mom is a symbol of feminism cannot even be debated; she is.

This is all to say that Collina and I share a similar anger when confronted with the idea that having babies or staying home as a mother is an anti-feminist notion. So when Collina found out she was pregnant while working in England, she knew *exactly* what she wanted. She wanted that baby. Unfortunately, the combination of her boyfriend's negative response, the lack of resources, and a spiritual mindset that she was continuing to grapple with, Collina found herself, alone, getting an abortion in her 20s. As I sat in our Gender and the Law class discussing Collina's story, I wondered how I would have reacted, as many women do. "I didn't have a choice," she professed; because for many women, there is no choice. You either must bring your pregnancy to term because of lack of geographic or economic access, or perhaps you fear what future you could provide at your current stage with your current network and so you feel as if abortion is your only option. A plethora of women fall along this scale. I, however, am blessed to have fallen in love with feminism in a way that brought me to Queer Theory, Sexuality Studies, Sexual Politics, and other forums of education that exercise my sexual knowledge in a way where I feel more prepared each day; but that is not to say that I do not fear daily that I might wake up on the scale where Collina and other women have. It is also why women like us recognize that this issue is exclusively about gender, as the ones who are the most fearful are the ones whose pregnancy tests scan positive, or whose birth control pills grow more expensive, or whose shame around purchasing Plan B expands.

*   *

La vie est trop courte pour s'épiler la chatte.

—ANONYME

Translation: *Life's too short to shave your pussy.*

—ANONYMOUS

*   *

PART III

The three of us were crowded around my bathtub, chuckling.

"Duuuude you *have* to shave. That seriously looks like a TREE."

I started shaving all the hair from my body in 7th grade. My sister taught me that I should use conditioner only on my ends, and showed me how to hold the razor against my legs to avoid cuts.

My male classmates had fur rugs for legs, and yet I was laughed at by a gang of middle school backwards hats because the cotton from my black T-shirt rested on my armpits. So I shaved; almost every other day, in fact. If I noticed the thin hair peeping out of my long pants during the winter, my chest would tighten. Winter dances meant swapping turtlenecks for exposed armpits; another trip to CVS to buy that Intuition branded razor that was meant for smoother legs.

My mom didn't like that I shaved my pubic hair, though, because maybe that meant people were seeing me undressed that weren't my sisters and close girl friends. But see every time I wore a bathing suit, someone could maybe see. I was embarrassed, and ashamed of the hair growing on my body.

A *Harper's Bazaar* ad released in 1922 read:

Without Embarrassment
An Intimate Talk to Women

The fastidious woman today must have immaculate underarms if she is to be unembarrassed.

This call to armpits was a product of the changing fashion industry; a change from near-complete concealment to sleeveless tops.

By the 1940s, *Harper's Bazaar* was not only targeting women's armpit hair, but their exposed legs as well. The numbers went from 66% of the ads mentioning leg hair, to 100% with 56% of those ads having leg hair as the focus.

In 1941 the 'zine wrote, "If we were dean of women, we'd levy a demerit on every hairy leg on campus."

The summer before my junior year of college, I forgot my razor at home while moving to yellow walls in DC Too lazy to spend the $9.99 on a razor pack from CVS, I chose to let my hair grow. Over the past year, I have gone from arms tight against my body and long sleeve shirts to tank tops and arms up complemented by my light brown under arms.

My housemate told me about Harriette Co. last week, and I entered a world of women not confined by their hair. Fresh Fur: Natural Deodorant. Magic Carpet Cleaner: Pubic Hair Shampoo. Bush Oil. Fringe Balm. These products are a reclamation of what is ours as women: fucking body hair.

My brothers-in-law always laugh when comparing their armpit hair next to mine. It's funny, it makes something powerful also silly; but I think the perk of a mark such as body hair on a woman invites curiosity. Maybe that curiosity takes the form of the boy across from me at lunch *staring* at my arms; or my brother in law chuckling at the length of my hair; or my roommate scrunching her nose when I hold the handrail above in a Lisbon metro.

My body hair led me to 100 Florida Avenue NE in DC on Sunday, December 3, 2017. Harriette Co. products can be found in three stores, and one happened to be Femme Fatale, a pop up shop open until Christmas Eve of this year. On this day the space was hosting Warrior Womban: A Preventative

Self-Care Expo. My friend Emily and I came about an hour into the session, greeted by grunts from a self-defense workshop, smells of vegan bean burgers, and warm smiles of femme entrepreneurs. Before stumbling upon the product that had reeled me in, I was drowning in embroidered uteruses, boob mugs, body butter, and vintage clothing. Tiptoeing amongst these 50+ businesses, all femme run, felt like a haven.

After an afternoon of artistic ambiance, juice demos, and falafel tastings, I felt a sense of strength as Emily and I left the venue. Multiple woman thanking *me,* of all things, asking if they'd see me again. On this day, I felt special because of a womanhood that has shown me a world of colorful voices, artwork, and stories. So thank you, *Harper's Bazaar,* for publicizing a trend that later made me a rebel, for encouraging my choice of growing armpit hair, both actions that brought me to a little pop up shop on Florida Avenue.

CHAPTER 9

———

This chapter is a love story to female blood and badass women in chronological order.

*   *

When it comes to swag, there's no gender involved.

—YOUNG THUG

*   *

PART I

You have one year to train for 26.2 miles.

But let's rewind four years. She is a Math major. Certain nights she plays at 18th Street Lounge, losing herself to drums whose beats excite a crowded bar.

Two years pass. She has succeeded as the first digital analyst for Interscope Records, and is simultaneously moving towards an M.B.A at Harvard Business School while also touring with M.I.A.

Kiran Gandhi was pursuing "the female archetype as an alternate source of leadership." She did not subscribe to a masculine stereotype of dominance—one of aggression defined by the loudest voice. Gandhi channeled an emotional intelligence that allowed for collaboration, balance, and eventually, an honest blog that blew up her voice.

It is 2015, and it is the 26.2 mile marathon in London. With yet another monument ahead, Gandhi gets her period. Afraid of the discomfort from a tampon, the chaffing with a pad, and a lack of knowledge of a menstrual cup, she decided the best choice was to free bleed; having not run with any other feminine product, there existed little to no choice.

"My ignorance made me feel like free bleeding was the best choice. . . [it was] a mixture of fear as much as it was radicalism." Mile by mile, Gandhi went with the flow (no pun intended). Feeling like a badass upon crossing the finish line was immediately contrasted by an influx of mass misogyny: how unhygienic, disgusting, another feminazi preaching about some sort of bullshit oppression.

"Oh, so you're another one of those feminists."

So this is when Gandhi got creative. She responded in a literal way, discussing how, actually, period blood is not unsanitary and is a part of a monthly routine for many women; "it isn't Carrie at the Prom," it's a vagina. To take the backlash at face value rather than as a theoretical discourse, Gandhi deconstructed each criticism masked behind a username with intelligence; and not only did she confront those against her decision, but she served as an example for those behind her. For certain women, "it's easier for them to not talk about their own body [as a taboo subject] . . . it made it easier to talk about some crazy marathon runner. It made [conversation] very accessible."

At the end of the marathon, Kiran Gandhi did laundry.

So this dirtiness aspect that always seems to be married to periods—it used to haunt me. I recently finished the who Big Mouth, a Netflix Original animated series starring John Mulaney, Nick Kroll, Maya Rudolph, and Jenny Slate; so basically a stacked cast of comedians. The episode *Everybody Bleeds* follows this group of 13 year olds on a field trip to the

Statue of Liberty, where one of the main characters gets her period for the first time.

I think the brilliance in this episode is when she tells her closest guy friend what has happened. He proceeds to projectile vomit uncontrollably. The message, intentionally hyperbolic, is that we have engrained a gendered reaction of disgust with something so biologically frequent and normal. Big Mouth's genius comes from the ability to accurately reflect how we all felt during puberty, while also communicating the ludicrous sentiments (such as a repulsion toward periods) that begin to intertwine themselves with our every thought.

Dominique Christina, a famous slam poet, so eloquently discusses her reaction to her daughter's period and hoping she can reclaim this "dirty" action in "The Period Poem":

> There is a thing called the uterus. It sheds itself every 28
> days or so... The feminist politics part is that women
> know how to let things go. How to let a dying thing
> leave the body, how to become new, how to regenerate,
> how to wax and wane...
> ...But when your mother carried you, the ocean in
> her belly is what made you buoyant, made you possi-
> ble...the body whose machinery you now mock...
> it's possible we know the world better because of the blood

that visits some of us . . . it interrupts our favorite white
skirts and shows up at dinner parties unannounced.
Blood will do that. Period. And when you deal with
blood over and over like we do . . . well, that makes you
a warrior.

*   *

Feminism says
as a woman in my arena
you are not
my competition
as a woman in my arena
your light
doesn't make mine
any dimmer

—ASHLEE HAZE

*   *

PART II:

An ode to my roommate: a personal essay

It started September, 2014.

The Make It Your Life poster stared me in the face. We giddily hug, meeting each other for the first time outside of a Facebook chat box.

My roommate is a Finance major; I study Women's and Gender Studies. My roommate has been budgeting since her freshman year in high school where she worked at a bank; I wear my savings within a week to school.

My roommate taught me to be tough. She taught me that just because she doesn't like to talk in the morning doesn't mean she's mad. She taught me that just because I grew up with my housemates (being my sisters) on the phone at 2 AM while I was sleeping, doesn't mean I can do that to her. She taught me that just because she doesn't say I love you doesn't mean she doesn't love me. She taught me that badass is a pencil skirt, it is a bank teller, and it is late night videos since day one of college.

But most importantly, my roommate showed me how women can constantly inspire other women. No, I'm not going to send in an application to Goldman Sachs; and no, I still don't know what bonds are, really. But I do know that every night when we blow out the candles and say goodnight, I am among a feminist energy that keeps me safe and carries my dreams.

So, to you, roommate, I'd like to say thank you. Thank you for being your weird, goofy self that reminds me of the inflatable tube man outside of car dealerships when you move like a noodle. Thank you for giving me a template for my resume. Thank you for holding me in the darkest of moments. Thank you for telling me when I need to get my shit together (which is often). Thank you.

This is my love letter to you, because I would not be here without you. And I am comforted by that every day.

Cheers to our four years, roommate.

*   *

They tried to bury us. They didn't know we were seeds.

—DINOS CHRISTIANOPOULOS

*   *

PART III

"Become an egg on the ground." It was during Tiffany Tao's internship at THINX that she was asked to model for the day. The shoot was to show a woman using THINX's underwear product while sleeping. "They were like, 'we don't wanna show a woman snuggled up in sheets with her boyfriend...so just be there, be sleeping, like an egg, and have that convey a powerful statement." In a room surrounded by only women, there was a level of comfort that was tangible for a 20-year-old intern.

Tao was first exposed to THINX during OWN IT, a women's leadership summit here in DC, when she shared a stage with the Director of Marketing at THINX. The panel on advancements of women's health and beauty was Tao's exposure to a world of intentional language for women's empowerment.

A grapefruit, a dripping egg yolk. A fruit and an embryo that have become symbols for the woman's body. THINX took these images and plastered them on underground walls to be in the faces of all those taking the subway; and it worked. As New York City's Metropolitan Transit Authority's advertising contractor, Outfront Media succumbed to the patriarchal lens and denounced THINX's marketing ads; but this was the point. The woman's body is a taboo, not something to celebrate, right? Taboo stems from the Polynesian word *tupua* which means menstruation. Taboo *means* menstruation. Menstruation *means* taboo. We can cat call their curves but discuss their sexual organs or represent them with a fruit? Absolutely out of the question.

Each one of my sisters entered the world defined by a monthly "week of shame" on a holiday. Lauralee was Labor Day. Gracey,

Christmas. Maggie, Valentine's Day. Natalie, her birthday. So when Cinco de Mayo rolled around my 7th grade year, I was excited to join the club. I was surprised by the color. I thought it was supposed to be apple red, not russet. I nervously asked my mom what was going on in my underwear, and she chuckled. And that was it. Period.

THINX's mission is to provide access to discussions and physical products that break down a red taboo. Instead of avoiding white pants, choosing your oldest pair of underwear, or having the bathroom be your best friend, period-proof underwear allows you to just go about your day. As part of the content team, Tao was able to "put [her] hands on everything." So instead of a male-dominated corporation, such as Tampax or Platex, where women's actual needs fall through the cracks, THINX handed Tao russet play dough, where she discovered empowerment through periods.

*   *

I am not free while any woman is unfree, even when her shackles are very different from my own.

—AUDRE LORDE

*   *

PART IV

SPRING 2016

The topic of the week was how women are used as weapons within war. The International Relations professor was leading a great discussion on the gendered employment of women through actions of genocidal rape. That phrase in and of itself is unsettling, so you can imagine Tiffany Tao's multitude of emotions during an incredibly violent lecture. At the end of her freshman year, she realized something.

"I was reflecting afterward with my friend Michelle who was in the same class. [I realized] I have a lot of avenues on campus where I can talk about [these issues] in an academic sense. . . but there's no place on campus to talk about how it makes you *feel*." Everything surrounded structural consequences, but there was no forum, at least for Tiffany and

Michelle, that allowed for a free-for-all response of emotions to disturbing, difficult, or general gendered histories. "And that was the day we came up with Bossier."

As found on their website, Bossier is "Georgetown's 'zine (magazine) dedicated to publishing work by women and femme authors and artists, as well as promoting discourse about women's issues and experiences on campus and across the globe."

I first saw Bossier's icon while abroad a year ago. Red sunglasses with heart-shaped frames. The name and imagery immediately peaked my interest; and its cofounders Tiffany Tao and Michelle Dale have only continued to outdo themselves. One year later, they have gained a diverse following of femme readers and writers, with their fourth issue soon to be released. Spreads cover funky playlists, intimate poems, inspiring drawings, intersectional feminist book reviews, the list goes on. "I gravitate towards having that women-only community," giggled Tao when across from me, discussing her original plan to go to Barnard College. At Barnard, "the women's health center is only there to treat women; they don't have a student health center. It's a women's health center." Barnard had hooked Tao, but she quickly pivoted to Georgetown. So when faced with an opportunity space, Tao ran with it. Bossier created a space for Tao's original goals behind attending Barnard; and Bossier created a space for me. The following is an excerpt from a piece I wrote for their third online issue:

I still see his eyes sometimes, or at least I think I see them. They're incredibly blue; sometimes green depending on his shirt. I always liked that about his eyes, the way they changed color.

He used to go quiet, a silence that I could predict with my stomachaches. My back would slide down the passenger seat, my body shrinking to half its size. My touch was too affectionate, my words too vulnerable. Not in public, he would say. His hands on my tights in a history classroom. Not in public, he would say. His mouth on my neck in an estranged hallway. Not in public, he would say.

I spend every day promoting a feminist mission whose statements I could not hear when lost in misogynist expectations of a man whose body I first felt the night before the ACT, of all things.

In a classroom tackling gendered violence as a mechanism of genocide and other violence, two badass Georgetown students created a 'zine.

PART V

I call this one, Theory Saved Me.

*   *

Theory emerges from the concrete.

—BELL HOOKS

*   *

That line resonates and echoes in my head. I am a straight, cisgender, white woman who goes to Georgetown University. You could say privilege emanates from my skin. When I found theory, however, I saw it feed my personal experience and resonate in a way that I could not quite vocalize.

Theory saved me, when I saw five daughters, myself included, see a man's infidelity take on a monstrous form that made him a stranger. I saw a woman's personhood, so deeply rooted in a role—as wife, as mother, as partner—crumble into tears on aging skin.

Theory saved me. I sprinted to Reading Motherhood and International Women's Rights like it was the end of a track and field meet. They gave me personal, they gave me political, they gave me comfort. I gripped my low-income identity as an intersectional piece that I could share with others, specifically other women.

Theory saved me. I found myself holding Judith Butler's hand at work, making feminism more and more my sound like it is for theorest Sarah Ahmed. I got angry at home. I snapped in bars and threw Audre Lorde like a brick at ignorant voices.

Theory saved me. Under the guise of a dinner date my sister and brother-in-law handed me a reality that I had envisioned but had not quite internalized. A sense of pride that formed a toxic cloud of masculinity wrapped its tight arms around my father's neck, stole his breath, and took the ground out from under my feet. I flipped frantically to the pages of Intro to Sexuality Studies and Michel Foucault where my dad's gendered expectations of himself echoed. I grew sad again to envision a loneliness he must have felt.

Theory saved me. My body is more than what you see on the surface. My body, at age 21, is quite worn. Next to some king's daughter in an entry level Georgetown prerequisite I feel tired. But I have a hope that does not inhibit my action but writes essays and drives me to the polls. I have a womanhood that makes reading a form of friendship, and academia a sense of release.

Theory saved me. I wish it could have saved him.

PART VI

The words of Dianne Reeves ring in my head. I imagine her on stage in 1993, boldly claiming her stance as an endangered species. I sip her words like coffee:

I am an endangered species
But I sing no victim's song
I am a woman I am an artist
And I know where my voice belongs
I am a woman I exist
I shake my fist but not my hips
My skin is dark my body is strong
I sign of rebirth no victim's song
I am an endangered species
But I sing no victim's song
I am a woman I am an artist
And I know where my voice belongs
They cut out my sex they bind my feet
Silence my reflex no tongue to speak
I work in the fields I work in the store
I type up the deals and I mop the floors
I am an endangered species
But I sing no victim's song
I am a woman I am an artist
And I know where my voice belongs
My body is fertile I bring life about
Drugs, famine, and war, take them back out

My husband can beat me his right they say
And rape isn't rape you say I like it that way
I am an endangered species
But I sing no victim's song
I am a woman I am an artist
And I know where my voice belongs
I know where my soul belongs
I know where I belong

I continue to sip.

CHAPTER 10

———

Four short stories. One, a simple definition; another, a simple conversation, an open letter, and a glimpse into bad sex.

*   *

Maybe none of this is about control. Maybe it isn't really about who can own whom, who can do what to whom and get away with it, even as far as death. Maybe it isn't about who can sit and who has to kneel or stand or lie down, legs spread open. Maybe it's about who can do what to whom and be forgiven for it. Never tell me it amounts to the same thing.

—MARGARET ATWOOD, *THE HANDMAID'S TALE*

*   *

PART I

Grab 'em by the pussy.

Yes, you were foolish to think I wouldn't mention this infamous quote. Let's deconstruct his words, shall we?

Grab: defined by Google as "to grasp or seize suddenly and roughly."

'Em: according to Dictionary.com, an informal variant of them. This has no gender, and can be implemented to strip away context, and, in the case of the above quote, humanity.

Pussy: well, on Google Translate this is a cat. In middle school, I learned its usage as slang for my vagina and/or vulva (even though most do not know what that is).

So, he encouraged us to "seize suddenly and roughly" the vagina or vulva of someone whose name, gender, and humanity was left out of the quote. I ask the women reading this, does that sound pleasurable to you? And to the men I ask, is this something you would like to perform?

*   *

We hold these truths to be self-evident: that all men and women are created equal.

—DECLARATION OF SENTIMENTS,
SENECA FALLS CONVENTION 1848

*   *

PART II

SATURDAY, DECEMBER 2, 2017.

"Are you a feminist?"

"Yes, are you?"

"No, and here's why. Gosh I love to argue this stuff."

This was a brief conversation I had with a freshman boy from American University. I told myself to keep my cool. To be honest, if the adrenaline you get is being a devil's advocate to feminists, you're not going to rustle my feathers because, well, I digress.

"So I mean, it's the respect thing. Like, women have all equal rights but they don't have respect. So like it's just about respect you know?"

So I say, "okay, so think about it this way. Sure, on paper you might view it as women and men having equal rights. But that doesn't mean that's how it plays on in real life. Also, feminism is more than just a dichotomy of men and women." I was going to go on to describe the idea of intersectionality, but I don't think he knew what dichotomy meant, so I paused to let him respond.

He responds and talks about waitresses and restaurants and how they are hired strictly because of their bodies. He points to mine. I tense up. I think he mentioned voting for Trump, perhaps I'm extrapolating based on his lack of linguistic intelligence combined with the Mango Juul attached to his lips.

This is not to say that I am unable to have a conversation with the other side, as I definitely am. But it is to say that many a times in order to devalue the other we criticize their personhoods rather than their argument. To attack my status as a feminist feeds into this idea of the "Angry Feminist Trope" a term coined by Barbara Tomlinson that basically gets at how we have a painted picture of some angry, hairy, masculine person who identifies as a feminist and hates all men; if he, however, had asked about my beliefs, rather than putting at my curves, I might have been able to stand longer than I did.

*   *

The behavior of a human being in sexual matters is often a prototype for the whole of his other modes of reaction in life.

—SIGMUND FREUD

*   *

PART III

An open letter to the Male Libido:

> You are infuriating, and so are your hosts. *The New York Times* article put it best, you live in men "of all different varieties, in different industries, with different sensibilities, bound together, solely, by the grotesquerie of their sexuality." So, you're not just living inside the kid from my high school who now exists in some toxic fraternity bubble at a liberal arts school, you're everywhere. *I* knew that. We as *women* knew that. But your nature as ever-present in all men is finally coming out to play re: the domino effect of sexual violence scandals.

> Your force takes form in a symbol so hastily drawn on white boards during study hall across the nation, and probably the world. Its shape resembles that of the Monument, and honestly so many other structures because the world

is phallic let's just face it. Your force hurts a lot of the time, by the way.

Michel Foucault talks about you, do you feel special? He paints the spirals of power and pleasure and the way sex is the emblem of this many-a-time problematic relationship.

You have been largely overlooked until now. Again, we knew you were around, but you have been historically reduced to moments, not as a participant in an oppressive pattern.

I met you first in middle school, when you encouraged that guy to touch me without asking in the hallway.

You're not bad in and of yourself, it is the ways in which we have construed you, stretched you, defined you, and implemented you as a weapon infused by desire that has become the evil. Your roots have defined language and action when it comes to power structures between a man and a woman, the heteronormative model.

To put it bluntly, ML, you are a jerk. And we will not stand for the misuse of desire, and the ways in which your hosts channel notions of you and masculinity.

'. . . But the point of Freud was not that boys will be boys. Rather the opposite: The idea of the Oedipus complex contained an implicit case for the requirements of strenuous repression: If you let boys be boys, they will murder their fathers and sleep with their mothers.'

All the Best,

Abigail

*   *

If we don't reclaim the narrative of our own experiences, somebody else will write that narrative for us.

—MADAME GANDHI

*   *

PART IV

I get a text from my friend Ali: "Omg have you read the *New Yorker* article called 'Cat Person.' You MUST."

She immediately follows this exclamation with a link to the article and a link to a response to the article. I put down everything I'm working on and start to read.

The story is simple. Boy meets Girl. Flirtation, sexual tension, movie date. It ends with bad sex. Not sexual violence or sexual harassment, but a girl thinking prioritizing the man's pleasure over her own distaste or growing hesitancy to have sex. It reads:

> Margot recoiled. But the thought of what it would take to stop what she had set in motion was overwhelming; it would require an amount of tact and gentleness that she felt was impossible to summon.

In responses to this article, they underline just that. That this story is one that I know many of my peers have felt or observed. A situation that you "willed," a flirtation you pursued, a night you might have even wanted to happen; but when you get there, to a so-called finale, you realize it is not what you wanted. The effort, however, that it would take to explain why you don't want to have sex or what cause this change feels like too much. So you just do it. You get it over with. And this is our *bodies* we're talking about.

I thought of these stream of consciousness when talk of Aziz Ansari spiraled after someone spoke out about his inappropriate actions. And I will say that I have mixed feelings of the incident; but the idea here is the same as what I write above. It doesn't have to be sexual harassment or assault to be sexist. Ansari constantly coming onto a woman who has been clear with him about what she wants is unfair. But our desires as women are often ignored. That is the message of Cat Person.

There's a British dark comedy called *The End of the F***ing World*. It's one of those short series that makes you laugh out loud and surprises you pretty constantly. It's quite odd; naturally, I loved it.

There's a scene in the middle of the first season that strikes me, that the story Cat Person is speaking to. The main girl, Alyssa, has brought a guy up to the room where she's staying and has blatantly announced to him that she would like to have sex. Mid-hookup, Alyssa stops and says "I'm sorry, but I changed my mind I'm not into this." The rest of the conversation goes like this:

> BOY: Are, are you kidding?
> ALYSSA: No.
> BOY: *Sighs.* That's not fair!
> ALYSSA: Uh . . . yes it is.
> BOY: *He inches closer to her.* Please, Alyssa. I think you are amazing."
> ALYSSA: Well then, respect my change of mind and fuck off please.
> BOY: *Storming out.* There is a word for girls like you!
> ALYSSA: I'll bet.

It's even more brilliant with the British accents.

The guy is stunned that she would decide she is not longer into their encounter, that she would even think to send him home or not want to have sex anymore. His reaction is to allude to calling her a degrading name and storm out like a child. Just as in Cat Person, the guy's reaction to Alyssa's lack of communication after their sex is to frequently text her and, after getting no responses, ending his side of the texting with: "Whore."

In reading a response to the article on *Man Repeller*, I was struck by one sentence in an all-encompassing way:

> When a woman fails to play her part, how quickly a 'nice guy' can turn.

We've seen this. With a partner who does not take well to the response "I'm tired" and does not find it to be a valid excuse to not have sex. With a guy you've met and you have to think of how to get out of the situation as to not irritate him if you decide you don't want to do anything. Because if you flirted, I mean, you lead him on, right? Well see that's where we have been taught to take on our contribution to this exchange and then prioritize a male's reaction, his desire, over our own. Because so quickly that friendly smile or good mood turns sour, and your heart hurts from hearing that awful word that ended the tale in Cat Person.

In response to Cat Person, I wrote my personal thoughts as a type of admittance to addiction. I am by no means *addicted* to male satisfaction, but at points in my life it has certainly felt that way. Because, whether good or bad, when I feel a certain male gaze—one that I overly criticize with feminist theory in a journal response—I stress a little less:

ADDICTED TO MALE SATISFACTION: A RESPONSE TO CAT PERSON

The snuggling is the best part. There's a relief that swarms over me when I get to relax; because, the unfortunate piece is that it's never about how I feel. I think they all want to think that's what they're doing—touching intentionally for the purpose of our pleasure. But how could it be, when their end is visible, and ours is ongoing?

I have an addiction to male satisfaction. I was bread to be this way. There's no particular place to focus blame. It was not the words of my parents, or even of my educators, but of a society that pushes reproduction, tells me "you're next" when the sister above me gets married, and questions my relationships with men.

The first time I got a taste of addiction was a lap around the track in Middle School P.E. Some boy wanted to be my boyfriend, and my cheeks got warm.

I continued to take them in like cigarettes.

My sophomore year in high school, I fell in like with a boy who was shy curly hair and my first drives alone with a license.

The second semester of the following, I fell in love with a boy whose eyes opened a world of goofy dancing, attic boardgames, and emotional outpour that suffocated me until I drowned.

The boy who made my cheeks warm still does.

My name is Abigail Glasgow, and I *was* addicted to male satisfaction.

CHAPTER 11

* *

Brother, when did you forget that the walls of a woman's body were once a fortress protecting you from a world you were too fragile for? She has been defending you long before you decided that she has no place defending you.

—JASMIN KAUR

* *

PART I

I mean, you're thirteen year old boys; pretty much everything that has to do with a penis or a vagina is funny. We all took [sex ed] super not seriously. . . it was a joke basically.

Ramsey, quoted above, is right. In many ways, the education our society provides to its students is a fucking joke; and when something is presented as a joke, it is carried out as a joke as well.

I went to a private school in Richmond, Virginia. So while Ramsey and I have different backgrounds in that respect, the attitudes towards sexuality, the female anatomy, and anything involving a penis or a vagina were about the same. I thought it was normal that I had been spanked by a majority of boys who I considered my friends. Yes, spanked. I remember being at recess and two boys staring blatantly at my boobs under my white shirt and pointing out the "titty dirt" that I had accumulated—i.e. a stain on my shirt that happened to be near my boobs. Each body part was reduced to a number—an arm, perhaps a 5 because it was too fat; a face, a 7 because it was hotter than some of the other girls. We, the girls, would play on a lower field, barricaded by a fence, while they, the boys, would give us a number. The attention my physical body received at age 13 was so much for my braces and skinny middle school legs that I got myself to the mall to make sure my boobs were up to the standards of my male counterparts. Because, after all, it was all a joke. At the time, I didn't question it. In fact, I didn't *really* care. I just wanted to be noticed and appreciated; but there was no thought of respect. There was spanking, objectification, and a loud "eww" if the idea of a period was mentioned. Instead of the graphic nature of a birth crowning engrained in a middle school boy's head, I have the sneers on my peers' faces when they took the joke of sexual education outside of the classroom, and used me as their demonstration.

Let me give you a glimpse of their demos.

"How many people did you make out with this weekend?"

"Well, two. But I mean it was dumb and for not that long."

"Slut."

FaceTiming with an old friend from high school, I asked what she recalled about these infamous study hall interrogations.

"I just remember you would walk into study hall and he would be like 'Hey Abigail, Zach or Jonathan?' It was always in front of everyone."

In 8th grade, we felt our changing bodies more tangibly than before: hiding in the corners of the locker room while changing, brushing our eyelashes with mascara, practicing close-mouthed smiles to cover braced teeth. So when I opened my mouth to someone else's on the tennis courts during the late night game's halftime, I forgot what it felt like to feel my body changing with no control. I liked to kiss. I liked the adrenaline on the football field before my mom came to pick me up, or the butterflies in the basement on a snow day. But according to my study hall mate, those feelings didn't matter, and I was a slut. His words would drown my confidence, his laugh would craft a large knot in my stomach. But I don't remember him doing this to the Zach or Jonathan, the two he so frequently questioned me about. They were allowed to do as they so pleased, but I was the slut. Slut. Slut. The word makes my eyes well up as I imagine so many girls' do when they hear the word for the first, second, or fiftieth time. He was my first experience with a sort of perpetrator. He now attends the University of Virginia, and probably could not recall this incident even if asked.

In 8th grade, I walked into Victoria Secret with the sole purpose of buying a level five pushup bra. I know, you probably had no idea that bras have levels. With each level comes more cushioning so that any woman can go from an A to a C with just one purchase, and not the surgical kind. I was 13, and I cared about my cleavage (or lack thereof) so much so that I actively pursued something to help rectify what I saw as a legitimate problem— that being that my body was not up to a defined standard.

To the boy who made her buy perfume because you teased her for her smell. To the boy who made her bleach what you deemed a mustache, because your sneers followed her down the hallway. To the boy who called her a prude because she made her own sexual choices. We see you, and we know you.

You're at the bar when we get home for Thanksgiving, talking to my mom at a neighborhood Christmas party. I hope you read this and understand what you did to us, because it didn't sit well. I have talked to many of my friends from home asking what they can remember from our K-12 private school experience. Mostly, it is the harsh words that follow us.

To the boys who made us question our worth, I want to say fuck you, but this isn't my personal journal. So to the educators, the parents, the older peers whose words mold those looking up to you: do better. Boys will not just "be boys"; girls who dress a certain way are not targets; and I am not a slut.

The word slut doesn't *really* have a definition. Hannah Witton, a british YouTube sensation and author, deconstructs the word in one of her popular videos entitled "Do I look like a Slut?"

Her point is, the definitions used are so contradictory. One generally attributes the word slut to a woman's sexual behavior, so then how can someone *look* like a slut? Witton looked to her audience via Tumblr, Facebook, and Twitter to decipher their definitions. These included but are not limited to:

- A social construct to uphold an unfair standard of women
- A derogatory term applied to women's behavior and dress code
- A human affected by double standards

- A word used to shame women's sexual agency
- A misogynistic concept
- Someone who uses sex to manipulate
- A woman who has sex with countless amounts of men
- What every man hopes a woman becomes when they are alone together

Witton concludes, after countless responses like those above, that the word in and of itself has no value. Unfortunately, however, attitudes contributing to such definitions above go beyond one harmful word.

Take the use of the word whore, for example. My sister pointed out to me that when used by itself, we automatically think woman; but if we are applying it to describe the actions or attitudes of a man, we add the gender to the word in order to distinguish—"man-whore." Whore by itself is automatically gendered.

With the progressive definitions, you get tangible outcomes such as the SlutWalk in LA, that, while controversial as many calls to action can be, served to bring together women and men alike in a march to end victim-blaming.

With the less respectful definitions, ones that sum up woman's identities by their relationship to sex with men, you get judge rulings based on women's clothing.

The comment that sparked the annual SlutWalk was from 2011, when police officer Michael Sanguinetti proposed safety advice to a select few students at Osgoode Hall Law School: "I've been told I'm not supposed to say this—however, women should avoid dressing like sluts in order not to be victimized."

In 2006, a judge in Manitoba ruled the defendant not guilty by noting the plaintiff's flirtatious attire—including a tube top and no bra.

Again in 2011, the governor of Jakarta, Governor Fauzi Bowo, responded to the rape and murder of an Indonesian citizen in a minivan by saying: "Imagine if someone sits on board a *mikrolet* (minivan) wearing a miniskirt; you would get a bit turned on."

Justice Robin Camp of Alberta resigned in March of 2017 after backlash against his comment, asking a victim why she can't "just keep [her] knees together?"

These gut-wrenching quotes and attitudes spiral from a label in a 7th grade classroom. An unpleasant study hall for me is a horrifying courtroom case for others; and the construct of slut, of assuming sexual agency over a woman's body because of the way she is dressed, is an ever-present companion.

But these attitudes and actions all start with language—of

how we view the victims. A favorite quote of mine by Jackson Katz—educator, author, and founder of the violence prevention and education program entitled Mentors in Violence Prevention–perfectly encapsulates the problem with language around gendered violence and language:

> We talk about how many women were raped last year, not about how many men raped women. We talk about how many girls in a school district were harassed last year, not about how many boys harassed girls. We talk about how many teenage girls in the state of Vermont got pregnant last year, rather than how many men and boys impregnated teenage girls...

> ...So you can see how the use of the passive voice has a political effect. [It] shifts the focus off of men and boys and onto girls and women. Even the term 'violence against women' is problematic. It's a passive construction; there's no active agent in the sentence. It's a bad thing that happens to women, but when you look at that term 'violence against women,' nobody is doing it to them. It just happens to them. Men aren't even [considered as] a part of it!

PART II

I was recently at the Renwick Gallery, about a week before Halloween, going to see Madame Gandhi perform. My friend Anita who had attended the same school as Gandhi in Manhattan, Chapin, came as my plus one. The two of us, both 21 years old, stood in a sea of real-life adults (their Halloween costumes, however, did make them less intimidating). The two of us in our matching antennas, as we were obviously aliens, decided to wait in the adult face-painting line, the obvious choice. While I sat on the bench in line, a man slid in a little too close to me while asking "mind if I sit here?" Well, yes, I do mind but at this point you're right next to me and people will think I'm an ass if I say "Yes sir I actually do mind." I stood up. Anita and I walked a few paces ahead, maintaining our ever-so-precious spot in line. "Ya know, my friend here really likes antennas. . . and there are two of you." Aah yes, the man sitting just a little too close decided to interrupt my waiting in line. ". . . he also likes side boob." Okay, so I have two options: turn around and destroy this man's ego in front of strangers, or, as is custom for many women who have been in this position one hundred times a day, ignore the piece of shit. I chose the latter.

About two minutes later, however, my dear POS decided to re-insert himself. This time, he cut to the chase. "SIDE BOOB." I chose the former.

"Sir, can you not? I am sitting here, minding my own business with my friend in line. Now that you have chosen to objectify my body in public, I am self-conscious about the side of my tank top. How old are you anyway? I am 21 years old and you look about 40. Please think before you speak."

"Uhh . . . I mean uhh it was my friend."

That was the response. "It was my friend."

And, ironically, Kiran Gandhi's Future is Female hit was playing in the background. Two Georgetown women confronting yet another androcentric mindset.

At the end of the night, I went up to Gandhi to congratulate her on a badass performance, give a hug, and go home with Anita. We were walking out, and POS from earlier ran to catch up.

"I just wanted to say I'm sorry. You know, I have a sister." Great. I have four. What is your point?

"I guess I'm just thinking about why I felt the need to scream that stuff. I mean, it was my friend who said it, but still I know it isn't cool."

"Thank you. I appreciate your apology. Maybe next time you go to say something about a stranger's body, you'll think about this moment."

"I absolutely will."

Anita and I ran to our Uber screaming "WE'RE CHANGING THE WORLD!"

And we were. We are.

CHAPTER 12:
DEAR GRACE

———

My niece is four years old. When she was first born, I sat in a corner of the hospital room bundled in February gear; and I cried. She was my sister and my brother in law wrapped up in a blanket and small knitted hat.

Much to my oldest sister's dismay, my niece and I now have a game we play sophisticatedly entitled "Booby Party." The game is simple: we jump up and down yelling booby party while pointing at our chests; it's our way of celebrating our womanhood.

"Seriously Abigail she's going to start screaming that at preschool and get in trouble," my oldest sister laughed.

We didn't start this game (it's honestly a fun chant) so that I could get my niece put in preschool detention. It was a funny little thing that came along as a way for me to share in my 22 year old feminism with my sister's 4 year old daughter.

So when my mom gave my niece a story book called *Goodnight Stories for Rebel Girls*, I saw the seed planted for a four year old feminism that made my eyes water like the first day I met her.

So I've decided to preface the conclusion of my book with a letter to my oldest niece, Grace. She has yet to be molded, and with every song she makes up and book she pretends to read because she has it memorized, she reminds me of me, and her mom, and her three other aunts. She's gonna do real things out there.

* *

Dear Grace,

When I first saw your picture, I was at a basketball game. You were a little peanut who looked exactly like your dad. I bragged about you pretty constantly. I thought it was low key super cool that I was a senior in high school while simultaneously an aunt. It was like I had joined some new little club and received an unspoken status increase.

You are the reason my snapchat was ever or has ever been popular. Random people would comment on my videos because of your little squeal or your routine where you point at your eyes, then your head, then your ears, then your mouth, then your belly button. I think I have that video memorized; I think there are a few people who do not share blood with us who also have it memorized just because I have made them watch it.

The video of you singing Jesus Loves Me, and Jingle Bells, and Rolling, and literally any other song known to humans gets me through my day. I have a video of you saying "I love you Abigail" that I would play every day in Senegal just to *feel* home.

I am so proud of your energy. You light up a room whether you look like Mowgli from the Jungle Book's twin while running around outside or you're in your best costume riding in the family wagon. I remember when you were around two years old, you heard the noise of a lawn mower and immediately said "dad!" because you knew when you heard that sound at home your dad was outside so you associated the two. That was one of many days where I saw how smart you are. I love perusing your mind and asking what you think about the world. You are brilliant. I know sometimes I give you sass, but that's because I know you can take it.

You have a responsibility that you have to uphold as the second sassiest daughter in our lineup of kids (me being the sassiest, of course).

Firstly, know that your parents rock; and even though I fight with them about politics every time I enter the house, I love them so much. Respect them; but also ask them questions. Question your environment; this brings me to my second point.

Understand that the reality handed to you is not the reality that everyone receives. Seek out others who are *different* than you are. You are special. It's exciting to navigate yourself in a crowd of people who do not resemble you. You'll learn a lot, I promise.

Thirdly, use that LOUD and powerful voice (sometimes, as of late, it's a bit of a shriek) to reach others with your ideas. Share your opinions with anyone who wants to listen, and listen to others. You are bold. Don't let anyone stop you from being and doing. Stick up for everyone like they are Noelle, our littlest Glasgow/Allen girl. Treat every human with the protection and kindness that you have for your little sister; trust me, life is much more fun that way.

Be the protection of Lauralee; the comfort of Gracey;

the boldness of Maggie; the sass of me; and the endless love of Natalie.

I love you my sweet Grace. I am so lucky for you to be the first young one I have been able to watch over, and I can't wait until you read this (IF your mom lets you . . .) and realize how crazy your aunt Abigail really is.

Be a badass forever, just like your mom, okay?

All my love,

Aunt Abigail

CHAPTER 13:
DEAR DAD

———

Dear Dad,

So, apparently I have just written a book. I wish you could read it; I really think you would like it. I'm sitting in this café in downtown DC, it's called Big Bear Café, and I'm trying to picture your face.

I got a package in the mail two days ago of some of your things. My favorite was your hat, because the inside smells like you.

This book is not meant to defame you; in fact, it's my way of best explaining you in a way that keeps your laugh in my heart, because now I think I know what could have steered you away at points.

I think your dad was unkind. I only met him that one time when I think I was maybe 7 and he smelled like smoke and seemed charming. From stories I have acquired of his personhood over the years, I think he set you up to fail. He passed along a value of masculinity and pride that made you believe *that* is what you're worth. So when your teacher told you you had beautiful legs "for a woman," you searched for power elsewhere. You found money. I think that Bible verse about love of money being the root of all evil should be a poster.

You met a beautiful woman; I know you loved her. She is beautiful. I think she made you forget about your dad's words, at least for a little.

Then you had us.

I remember everyone telling me I was like you, and that felt *so* good. You were brilliant, and you were kind. There was one night in high school—I think sophomore year—where I had this horrible panic attack. I used to get those because there was a level of perfection I was trying to achieve and I felt worthless that I couldn't. You came upstairs and found me, and you held me. I know you loved me.

When you told us what happened with another woman, I lost feeling in my body. You had been my idol, and now you were just a human being. I felt hurt, and I hurt the most for mom, because she didn't deserve *any* of that; but this letter is about you.

I feel sad for you, because somewhere along the way you lost this sense of pride, filtered through a crafted, masculine lens, and you left us. How lonely that must have felt, and I wish I could have changed that.

In the package of your things, there was a hand-made book I had given you. It was called, "How to Keep Your Head Up," my first sense of authorship. I cried when I read the letter I wrote you in that book. I told you you would see me graduate, you would walk me down the aisle, and you would know my children. That day I realized none of those things will happen. Today I again realize none of those things will happen.

I am sorry societal norms and expectations drowned you in what you thought you should be. I am sorry they made you believe your life was not worth living, because I know that it was.

I grew up so proud of my middle name because it was your name. Then, two years ago, I wanted to erase that middle name because you hurt me. Now, I will wear your name with a new pride; not one of masculinity and power, but one of kindness and empathy. I will take the gentle pride that I know you felt for me, and I will transform it for the world.

I have six tattoos now. Yeah yeah I know, you wouldn't hire me. But I think we always knew I was going to rebel. One is of a bird on a wire with another flying above the wire; it's supposed to be you and me. So I wrote a poem called Birds on a Wire about you, it was for a graphic design project. I'm writing a thesis about you, too. It's about toxic masculinity and mental health. As you can see, I'm using your story to inspire me. I hope that's okay.

When I smoke a cigarette alone outside, I always feel you. I don't know why, but I do. It's special. Not good for my lungs, but special.

I love you, Dad. I will miss our FaceTimes where I yelled at you for not voting, and you told me I should read more than just *VICE* and the *New York Times*. Thank you for your wisdom, and your faults. You changed my life forever, and I hope to change others with you always in the back of my mind.

With all my love, until we meet again,

Abigail

CHAPTER 14:
DEAR MOM

———

Dear Mom,

I wanted to end my book with you. As I sit here, I am overwhelmed with words for you; simultaneously, I am speechless.

I used to come home upset, because I wore this sparkly pink poncho from Limited Too and people made fun of me. Instead of gossiping with me and saying that person was stupid, you asked me what they could be experiencing to make them belittle someone else. Sometimes, your role as devil's advocate would infuriate my elementary school self; now, I am so grateful. You taught me how to know others, how to read people; you taught me how to be kind.

I don't think you have ever asked anything of any of us. You bent over backwards for the happiness of 6 humans, and you didn't ask for one thing. I am angry at my high school self that left the kitchen to do a calculus pledge set instead of helping you load the dishwasher. When I talk to strangers, I speak with you in my head; I hope that can sort of make up for the numerous forks I didn't load.

I have never met a person like you. I'm sure many say that about their mom, but I think they might be wrong; because *no one* is like you. No one knows the Westbury Pharmacy cashier's story about Easter baskets. No one takes in a friend's granddaughter as another child when they already have five of their own. No one defines a home like you do, knows God like you do, and imparts wisdom like you do.

"You feel *just the same*."

I love when you say that, because sometimes I don't feel as if I feel just the same. I know I'm a cynic that talks about genocide on Thanksgiving and vocalizes a distaste for the Robert E. Lee statue on Monument Avenue, and I can hear my voice become angry when I speak about our world. I hope you know it's never anger toward you, it's anger for you. Because you were handed a set of truths that could have debilitated you, and you wake up every morning, which wakes me up every morning. So, you see, when I think of marginalized people who are handed a set of truths beyond their control that society has deemed less than, I think of you. Because you are the reason I do not complain about an ugly set of truths handed to me, but instead I think of those who crafted those horrible truths, and why they might have done that. You are the reason I still love my dad, when he was the creator of our broken family.

You changed my life the day you made me realize that the person who made fun of my sparkly poncho was unkind for a reason. You taught me how to channel anger into empathy, even now when I forget and scream "fuck Mike Pence" during family dinners (for the record, I still do not like Mike Pence).

I'm no math major, but after googling "what is the probability of having five children of the same gender," and pretending that I still remember high school algebra and calculus, I would dare to say that the odds we ended up with our family—five children of the same gender— come to 3.125%. So not only intuitively, but mathematically, growing up as one of five daughters is uncommon. And you nailed it. You really did.

I don't know how to eloquently construct this letter, because my mind jumps to so many stories of you. The story of your chapter idea talking about the point in your life where your purse or bag had diapers for your newborn and tampons for your 14 year old. The story of you seeing all 8 shows I performed of *Annie* when I was in 6th grade. The story of you hugging the guy in my grade who other moms deemed a "bad egg." The story of you watching movies with me all day alongside Eggo Waffles when my forehead hit 102 degrees. You aren't a mom. You are Rostov's warm coffee, you are Jesus Loves Me, you are tears and long hugs and late night discussions. You are a woman whose light turns people around, and I am the most blessed to feel that.

You are a badass. You are valuable. And you are loved by a girl who wants to change the world for you. I hope I do, my sweet mom. Because I know you will.

My vision of this book started and ended with you.

I'll be home soon mom.

Lysm my Lu,

Abigail

ACKNOWLEDGMENTS

Thank you to those who shared their stories with me—from vulnerable to comedic—in an effort to help me intertwine my own story; and to women whose words found themselves on my pages or in my head because of their power.

Thank you to my siblings for putting up with my antics whenever I come home and rant about feminism and its current state.

Thank you to friends who listened to chapter excerpts and ideas and who love me even though I'm definitely not normal.

Thank you to Rachel Whelan for four years of you.

And thank you to my parents, for different reasons.

To my dad for challenging me, and proving that I know how to love unconditionally.

And to my mom for being the ultimate feminist. *My* ultimate feminist.

REFERENCES

___

Bay-Cheng LY, The trouble of teen sex: the construction of
adolescent sexuality through school-based sexuality education, *Sex Education: Sexuality, Social and Learning*, 2003,
3(1):61–74.

Cai, Weiyi, and Scott Clement. "What Americans Think
about Feminism Today." *Washington Post—Kaiser Family
Foundation Poll. The Washington Post.* 27 Jan. 2016.

"Do I Look Like a Slut?" *YouTube*, uploaded by Hannah Witton,
www.youtube.com/watch?v=I3bQLq9QGA4. 28 Oct. 2014.

France, Lisa Respers. "#MeToo:Social media flooded with
personal stories of assault." *CNN*, 16 Oct. 2017. www.cnn.
com/2017/10/15/entertainment/me-too-twitter-alyssa-mi-
lano/index.html.

George, Beth, and Ron Blome. "Sex Education in Public Schools."
Louisiana Digital Media Archive, 27 April 1979,

http://ladigitalmedia.org/video_v2/asset-detail/LSWI-0284-02_InDepth. Accessed 26 Feb. 2018.

"Guttmacher Institute State Policies Brief." *Guttmacher Institute*, www.guttmacher.org

"Joe Biden Says It's on Men to End Rape Culture." *Refinery29*, 12 Jan. 2017.

Nahman, Haley. "'Cat Person' Tells a Story Most Women Know About Bad Sex." *Man Repeller.* 12 Dec. 2017.

Nathanson CA, *Dangerous Passage: The Social Control of Sexuality in Women's Adolescence*, Philadelphia: Temple University Press, 1991.

Njambi, Wairimu Ngaruiya. 'One Vagina To Go.' Australian Feminist Studies. 2009, pp. 167-180.

Mohanty, C. *Under Western Eyes.* 1988. 30: 61.

Roupenian, Kristen. "Cat Person." *The New Yorker*, 11 Dec. 2017.

Schneewind KA, Socialization and education: theoretical perspectives, in: Smelser NJ and Baltes PB, eds., *International Encyclopedia of Social and Behavioral Sciences*, Amsterdam: Elsevier, 2001, pp. 14507–14513.

"Sex Education: Last Week Tonight with John Oliver (HBO)." *YouTube*, uploaded by LastWeekTonight, 9 Aug. 2015. www.youtube.com/watch?v=LojQz6jqQSo. Accessed 26 Feb. 2018.

"The Camp Gyno." *YouTube*, uploaded by HelloFlo, 28 July 2013, www.youtube.com/watch?v=oXnzfRqkRxU.

Made in the USA
Middletown, DE
27 June 2018